The Civil War

⎡ OPPOSING
VIEWPOINTS®
DIGESTS ⎤

The Civil War

DAVID M. HAUGEN AND LORI SHEIN

Greenhaven Press, Inc., San Diego, California

Library of Congress Cataloging-in-Publication Data

Haugen, David, 1969–
    The Civil War / David Haugen, Lori Shein.
        p.   cm. — (Opposing viewpoints digests)
    Includes bibliographical references (p.   ) and index.
    Summary: Offers opposing viewpoints on issues associated with the Civil War including secession, slavery, the Emancipation Proclamation, and the President's right to suspend civil liberties.
    ISBN 1-56510-887-6 (lib. : alk. paper). — ISBN 1-56510-886-8 (pbk. : alk. paper)
    1. United States—History—Civil War, 1861–1865—Juvenile literature. [1. United States—History—Civil War, 1861–1865.] I. Shein, Lori, 1957— . II. Title. III. Series.
E468.H35   1999
973.7—dc21
                                                                    98-46105
                                                                        CIP
                                                                         AC

Cover Photo: National Archives
Archive Photos: 74
Dover Dictionary of American Portraits: 92
Library of Congress: 13, 17, 19, 20, 21, 23, 25, 42, 62, 69
Louis A. Warren Lincoln Library and Museum: 26
National Archives: 80
North Wind Picture Archives: 9, 45, 55

©1999 by Greenhaven Press, Inc.
PO Box 289009, San Diego, CA 92198-9009

Printed in the U.S.A.

CONTENTS

FOREWORD

The only way in which a human being can make some approach to knowing the whole of a subject is by hearing what can be said about it by persons of every variety of opinion and studying all modes in which it can be looked at by every character of mind. No wise man ever acquired his wisdom in any mode but this.

—John Stuart Mill

Greenhaven Press's Opposing Viewpoints Digests in history are designed to aid in examining important historical issues in a way that develops critical thinking and evaluating skills. Each book presents thought-provoking argument and stimulating debate on a single topic. In analyzing issues through opposing views, students gain a social and historical context that cannot be discovered in textbooks. Excerpts from primary sources reveal the personal, political, and economic side of historical topics such as the American Revolution, the Great Depression, and the Bill of Rights. Students begin to understand that history is not a dry recounting of facts, but a record founded on ideas—ideas that become manifest through lively discussion and debate. Digests immerse students in contemporary discussions: Why did many colonists oppose a bill of rights? What was the original intent of the New Deal and on what grounds was it criticized? These arguments provide a foundation for students to assess today's debates on censorship, welfare, and other issues. For example, *The Great Depression: Opposing Viewpoints Digests* offers opposing arguments on controversial issues of the time as well as views and interpretations that interest modern historians. A major debate during Franklin D. Roosevelt's administration was whether the president's New Deal programs would lead to a permanent welfare state, creating a citizenry dependent on government money. *The Great Depression* covers this issue from both historical and modern perspectives, allowing students to critically evaluate arguments both in the context of their time and through the benefit of historical hindsight.

This emphasis on debate makes Digests a useful tool for writing reports, research papers, and persuasive essays. In addition to supplying students with a range of possible topics and supporting material, the Opposing Viewpoints Digests offer unique features through which young readers acquire and sharpen critical thinking and reading skills. To assure an appropriate and consistent reading level for young adults, all essays in each volume are written by a single author. Each essay heavily quotes readable primary sources that are fully cited to allow for further research and documentation. Thus, primary sources are introduced in a context to enhance comprehension.

In addition, each volume includes extensive research tools, including a section comprising excerpts from original documents pertaining to the issue under discussion. In *The Bill of Rights*, for example, readers can examine the English Magna Carta, the Virginia State Bill of Rights drawn up in 1776, and various opinions by U.S. Supreme Court justices in key civil rights cases, as well as an unabridged version of the U.S. Bill of Rights. These documents both complement the text and give students access to a wide variety of relevant sources in a single volume. Additionally, a "facts about" section allows students to peruse facts and statistics that pertain to the topic. These statistics are also fully cited, allowing students to question and analyze the credibility of the source. Two bibliographies, one for young adults and one listing the author's sources, are also included; both are annotated to guide student research. Finally, a comprehensive index allows students to scan and locate content efficiently.

Greenhaven's Opposing Viewpoints Digests, like Greenhaven's higher level and critically acclaimed Opposing Viewpoints Series, have been developed around the concept that an awareness and appreciation for the complexity of seemingly simple issues is particularly important in a democratic society. In a democracy, the common good is often, and very appropriately, decided by open debate of widely varying views. As one of democracy's greatest advocates, Thomas Jefferson, observed, "Difference of opinion leads to inquiry, and inquiry to truth." It is to this principle that Opposing Viewpoints Digests are dedicated.

INTRODUCTION

A Nation Divided

The Civil War was not an unexpected event in American history. The seeds of division between North and South had been planted decades before the outbreak of hostilities. From colonial times, Southern states had maintained an agricultural economy based on large plantations that produced cash crops such as cotton and tobacco. Because these crops required numerous laborers to harvest, the South relied on imported African slaves (more than 3 million on the eve of the Civil War). Although the North, too, grew grain in abundance on small farms in the Midwest, in the early 1800s New England had embraced the European Industrial Revolution and subsequently developed a manufacturing base. Industry gave the Northern economy room to grow and diversify. The Southern economy, on the other hand, was limited by available land and the maximum seasonal yield of its crops. One French visitor to the States noted,

> Every day [the North] grows more wealthy and densely populated while the South is stationary or growing poor. . . . The first result of this disproportionate growth is a violent change in the equilibrium of power and political influence. Powerful states become weak, territories without a name become states. . . . Wealth, like population, is displaced. These changes cannot take place without injuring interests, without exciting passions.[1]

Slavery: The Great Division

The growing political power in the North manifested itself through the emergence of a strong abolition movement that was bent on ridding the nation of slavery. Southerners, protecting their economy and way of life, were equally determined to defend the institution of slavery, though less than half owned slaves. The issue of slavery became a symbolic rallying point for both Southerners and Northerners. Those in the South who did not own slaves saw attempts to end it as a symptom of a much larger design to topple Southern culture. Most Northerners, who cared little about the fate of blacks, saw the threatened expansion of slavery into new territories as a Southern ploy to increase their influence in national policy. Primarily, neither group was genuinely concerned about the well-being of the African Americans laboring in bondage.

Slavery was only one of the issues that divided the Union. Like slavery, most of the divisive issues seemed to stem from a much larger contention over the power of the states versus

Slavery was one of the most hotly debated issues between the North and the South.

the authority of the central government. Southern grievances throughout the antebellum period were aimed at the growing influence of the central government over the states. Southerners feared what Senator John C. Calhoun of South Carolina termed the "increasing power of this Government, and of the control of the Northern section over all its departments."[2] If radicals in the North could transmit their ideals through Congress, then the South's social hierarchy and its economy would be imperiled. The agricultural South had already seen the industrial North push for a high tariff on imported goods; now Southerners were convinced that abolitionist schemes to end slavery were poorly disguised attempts to deprive the South of its labor pool.

The Balance of Power

Only Congress could enact legislation to abolish slavery, so Southerners tried to maintain a balance of representation in the Senate. If the North could not achieve a majority of congressional votes on abolitionist legislation, then slavery was secure. The North also felt the need for balance since it wanted to keep slavery from spreading unchecked. Contention between the two political forces eventually arose as Americans spread westward and new states were added to the Union. To maintain the congressional balance, acts were passed that allowed the admission of a free state (where slavery was not permitted) with the requirement that a slave state also be admitted. This balance was upset by the Compromise of 1850, which admitted California as a free state in exchange for a tougher fugitive slave law that made Northerners liable for returning runaway slaves. The majority of states in the Union were now free, the balance being tipped at sixteen to fifteen.

Early Martyrs

The next piece of legislation to address the spread of slavery in the United States was the Kansas-Nebraska Act of 1854.

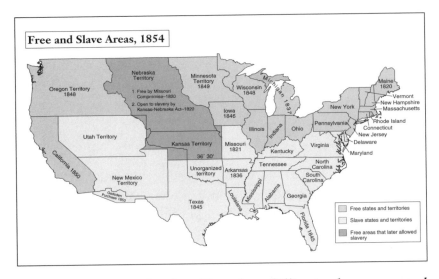

Pushed by Senator Stephen Douglas of Illinois, the act created the territories of Kansas and Nebraska and left it up to the residents of those would-be states to decide whether to permit slavery within their borders. Douglas proclaimed, "If the people of Kansas want a slaveholding state let them have it, and if they want a free state they have a right to it, and it is not for the people of Illinois, or Missouri, or New York, or Kentucky, to complain, whatever the decision of the people of Kansas may be."[3] Instead of reigning as a symbol of practical democracy, the Kansas-Nebraska Act fostered violence. Abolitionists and proslavery forces from other states converged on Kansas to try to influence the decision of the local residents. Threat and intimidation escalated to murder as small pitched battles occurred between the two factions. "Bleeding Kansas" symbolized the failure of compromise on the volatile issue of slavery.

Before the decade was out, more violence would erupt. In 1859 John Brown, an antislavery extremist, led a group of abolitionists and free blacks to Virginia and seized the federal arsenal at Harpers Ferry. Brown's plan was to start an armed slave rebellion in the South. Although Brown and his followers were captured and convicted of treason (Brown was hanged), the South interpreted this move as an indication that the North was willing to use armed force to end slavery. The abolitionists, on the other hand, had their first nationally recognized martyr. Upon hearing of Brown's fate, poet Henry David Thoreau wrote,

> If this man's acts and words do not create a revival, it will be the severest possible satire on the acts and words that do. It is the best news that America has ever heard. It has already quickened the feeble pulse of the North, and infused more and more generous blood into her veins and heart than any number of years of what is called commercial and political prosperity could. How many a man who was lately contemplating suicide has now something to live for![4]

Secession

In 1860 Abraham Lincoln was elected the sixteenth president of the United States. Lincoln vowed to confine his duties to those specified by the Constitution. He declared, "The power confided to me, will be used to hold, occupy, and possess the property, and places belonging to the government, and to collect the duties and imposts."[5] Southern leaders were not convinced of Lincoln's impartiality; he had run on an abolitionist platform and spoken against the extension of slavery. Southerners assumed his Northern supporters would expect some satisfaction. In response to Lincoln's election, the South Carolina legislature convened an emergency meeting in December and voted to secede from the Union. South Carolina defended its action by attesting that the states had the right and the power to leave the Union whenever their interests were threatened. In January 1861 five other states of the Deep South—Alabama, Florida, Georgia, Louisiana, and Mississippi—joined South Carolina, and the next month they formed the Confederate States of America. Mississippi senator Jefferson Davis was elected president of the Confederacy. In March, Texas seceded; that same month President Lincoln

The election of President Abraham Lincoln was viewed as a major threat to the Southern lifestyle. Immediately after he took the oath of office, several Southern states seceded from the Union.

delivered his inaugural address and declared that the rebel states did not have the power to dissolve the Union. The new president affirmed, "No state, upon its own mere motion, can lawfully get out of the Union,—that *resolves* and *ordinances* to that effect are legally void." Lincoln argued that, by accepting the Constitution, the states had willfully abandoned their sovereignty in order to claim the advantages of a strong central government. Lincoln made it clear that he would use his office to preserve the Union, including meeting any threat employed against federal installations in the South. "Acts of violence within any state or states against the authority of the United States are insurrectionary or revolutionary, according to circumstances."[6]

In April 1861 South Carolina declared that all federal troops had to be evacuated from all parts of its sovereign territory. In Charleston's harbor lay the federal installation of Fort Sumter, an unfinished bastion that refused to heed South Carolina's orders. On April 12 Confederate gun batteries on shore opened fire on the fort. The defenders withstood a thirty-four-hour bombardment, but with no hope of aid, they surrendered. President Lincoln responded to the Southern aggression by calling for seventy-five thousand volunteers to fill the ranks of the Union army. Southerners interpreted this as an act of war, and Arkansas, North Carolina, Tennessee, and Virginia decided to join the Confederacy. With Virginia on their side, the Confederates moved their seat of government to Richmond in May.

Mobilizing for War

The president's mobilization of the Union army brought some criticism from Lincoln's detractors, who said that congressional approval was needed for such an action. Lincoln felt that the Constitution granted the president broader authority in times of war, and he followed up his call to arms with another unsponsored order to have the navy blockade Southern ports. When Southern sympathizers or antiwar protesters began to grumble about these acts, Lincoln suspended the right of habeas corpus and had authorities arrest and detain anyone suspected of obstructing the war effort. In Maryland, Mayor George Brown noted how this translated from word to deed: "If a newspaper promulgated disloyal sentiments, the paper was suppressed and the editor imprisoned. If a clergyman was disloyal in prayer or sermon, or if he failed to utter a prescribed prayer, he was liable to be treated in the same manner."[7] Again, Lincoln assumed this power to revoke habeas corpus was within presidential purview during times of extreme urgency, but his critics did not. Chief justice of the Supreme Court Roger B. Taney denounced Lincoln's measures as far exceeding his powers, but the president defended them as necessary to maintaining the war effort and saving the Union.

As both sides mobilized for war, volunteer regiments from small towns and large cities across the nation converged in the East. Some Union troops even came all the way from California to fight. The men of certain regiments, especially those from smaller towns, knew each other very well, and many of these regiments contained several men who were related. While brothers and cousins often fought alongside each other, they also occasionally fought against one another. Especially in the border states of Missouri, Kentucky, Maryland, and Delaware, as well as part of Virginia (which became the state of West Virginia), issues such as slavery often divided families. (Only Lincoln's declaration that the war was being pursued to preserve the Union and not to end slavery kept some of the border states from joining the Confederacy despite their tolerance of slaveholding.) The fact that these soldiers often knew each other and represented their hometowns kept many of them from displaying cowardice on the battlefield, though it did not ensure they would not rout en masse.

Confidence vs. Competence

Once the war began, the bravery of the troops would be promptly tested. Union armies immediately invaded the South and achieved some initial victories in small actions. Buoyed by their army's success, Northerners thought the war would be over quickly. At the First Battle of Bull Run (near Manassas, Virginia), the Union's overconfidence would be shattered. Politicians and townspeople came from Washington, D.C., to watch the Union

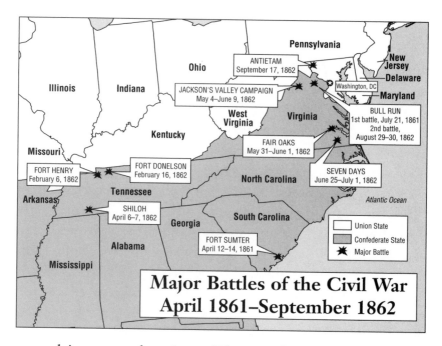

Major Battles of the Civil War
April 1861–September 1862

army claim yet another victory. They watched as the Union army initially swept the field, until Confederate general Thomas Jackson held his men firm and the rest of the Southern army rallied around his brigade. In a letter to his wife, Jackson confided, "Whilst great credit is due to other parts of our gallant army, God made my brigade more instrumental than any other in repulsing the main attack."[8] When the South counterattacked, the Union army routed and the legion of spectators was caught in a mad dash back to Washington. "Stonewall" Jackson had proven that the South would not be easily defeated.

The Southern armies under the command of Joseph Johnston followed up the battle at Manassas with other victories. Lincoln was desperate to turn the tide, so he looked to General George B. McClellan, the newly appointed general in chief of the Union army, to bring the war to the South by seizing the Confederate capital at Richmond. McClellan was slow to act, and his delays let the South gain valuable time to amass its armies. Lincoln became impatient with the inactivity, announcing at one White House war council meeting, "If General McClellan does not want to use

the Army, I would like to *borrow* it for a time."[9] Eventually Mc-
Clellan pressed toward Richmond but, constantly overestimating
the strength of the enemy's troops, he refused to commit all of the
troops under his command and was constantly beaten off by Johnston, once only six miles from the capital. Johnston was wounded
in one engagement and was replaced by General Robert E. Lee.
A brilliant tactician, Lee crushed a Union army during the Battle
of the Seven Days and then invaded Maryland. McClellan moved
to intercept the Confederates at Sharpsburg. In the battle that ensued, two thousand Union troops and twenty-seven hundred
Southerners lay dead near a small creek called Antietam. September 17, 1862, would remain the costliest day of fighting in the war.

Freeing the Slaves

Since Lee withdrew his forces from the field at Sharpsburg,
Union propagandists were quick to claim a victory. Lincoln had
been waiting for such an opportunity. On September 22 he issued a preliminary version of the Emancipation Proclamation,

*Several thousand troops lay dead after a battle at Antietam, Maryland. This bat-
tle had the highest death toll for any day of fighting during the entire Civil War.*

which granted freedom to slaves held in Confederate states (interestingly, it did not mention slaves held in the border states). The Emancipation Proclamation was not a law; it was a war measure that could be overturned by Congress. It was also not an enforceable piece of legislation. In effect, the majority of slaves were still behind Confederate lines, unable to walk away from Southern plantations regardless of whether the proclamation declared them free. Although Lincoln's altruism was probably sincere, the proclamation was, at least in part, designed to ensure that enlightened nations like England and France could not justify entering a war against a government that had condemned slavery. Lincoln feared foreign intervention but was assuaged when men like English social critic John Stuart Mill publicly acknowledged the social justice of Lincoln's act. Mill wrote, "The triumph of the Confederacy would be a victory of the powers of evil which would give courage to the enemies of progress and damp the spirits of friends all over the civilized world."[10] In issuing the proclamation, however, Lincoln received heavy criticism from Northerners who remembered that Lincoln had attested that the war was being fought to preserve the Union and not to free the slaves.

Turning Points

Between 1862 and 1863 the Union army was still not winning decisive victories in the East. Lincoln removed the sluggish McClellan from his command and tried a series of successors, all of whom proved to be just as ineffective. The South was having its own problems. Lee was winning battles, but at a terrible cost in lives that could not be replaced. At Chancellorsville in May 1862, Lee suffered more than twelve thousand casualties, one of which was his most capable general, Stonewall Jackson (who was shot accidentally by his own men). Southern armies were shrinking. They were also suffering the effects of inadequate supply. The Union blockade was working too well; few foreign munitions reached the Confederate coastline, and the South did not have the industrial capabilities to compensate. In

The Battle of Chancellorsville was responsible for twelve thousand Confederate deaths and helped the Union Army gain a valuable edge.

1863 Jefferson Davis's government issued the Impressment Act, which allowed Confederate agents to commandeer any civilian property deemed necessary to continue the war effort. Southerners lost food, livestock, and horses to the Impressment Act, but the measure was not enough. The Southern armies were forced to scavenge what they could from the battlefield or actively go in search of supplies in Union-held territory.

In June 1863 Lee's poorly supplied army pushed into Northern territory, entering southern Pennsylvania. By early July Lee's men approached the small town of Gettysburg in search of new shoes to replace the ones that had worn out after years of marching. Outside the town the advance brigades of the Confederate army encountered a Union cavalry detachment. The Army of the Potomac, under the new leadership of George G. Meade, had been following the Southerners for some time. The encounter turned into a fierce battle as more and more troops from both sides arrived on the field. The contest climaxed when Lee approved a reckless plan to

A major turning point in the Civil War was the Battle of Gettysburg, in which General Robert E. Lee ordered an uphill frontal assault led by General George E. Pickett. "Pickett's Charge" cost thousands of Confederate lives and diminished the South's chances of winning the war.

storm Union defenses in a massive frontal assault. Led by General George E. Pickett, the assault, which came to be known as Pickett's Charge, was costly and ineffectual. Lee accepted the blame for poor judgment, riding out to meet the survivors of the charge and confessing, "It was all my fault. Get together and let us do the best we can toward saving that which is left us."[11] Lee and his decimated army retreated to

Virginia. Gettysburg proved to be the turning point in the eastern campaign. The Confederates had lost too many men to launch any further large-scale assaults; they could only fight defensively while they were pursued by the growing Union army. President Lincoln visited Gettysburg shortly after the battle. He spoke a few words to a small crowd that had gathered. In this, his Gettysburg Address, Lincoln stated, "We here highly resolve that these dead shall not have died in vain—that this nation, under God, shall have a new birth of freedom—and that government of the people, by the people, for the people, shall not perish from the earth."[12]

The day after the Battle of Gettysburg, the Confederate stronghold of Vicksburg, Mississippi, fell to Union forces led by General Ulysses S. Grant. The fall of Vicksburg opened the Mississippi River to federal use. Grant had already shown himself a capable commander who understood that the war was a war of attrition: As long as more Southern troops perished than Northern troops, the North would win. In 1862 he had captured two Tennessee forts by demanding that the Confederate defenders surrender unconditionally, earning him the nickname "Unconditional Surrender" Grant. Later

Ulysses S. Grant

that year he sent the Southern army into retreat at Shiloh, Tennessee. These victories did not go unnoticed by President Lincoln, who was still looking for an aggressive general in chief. Lincoln appointed Grant to the position the following year.

Black Soldiers

One of the more historically relevant, though tactically uninteresting, battles of the war also took place in July 1863. The Fifty-fourth Massachusetts Volunteers, a regiment composed of black soldiers, stormed Fort Wagner in Charleston harbor on the night of July 18. Former slaves and free blacks enlisted in the Union army in large numbers after the Emancipation Proclamation indicated Lincoln's decision to utilize black troops. Although these men were paid less than their white counterparts and faced constant discrimination from Northerners who felt that this was a white man's war, blacks continued to fill the ranks. By war's end, about 180,000 African Americans served in 166 all-black regiments (these units, however, were commanded by white officers). Most of these regiments were given noncombat duties; only a few saw action, which prompted the rumor that the black troops were not skilled enough to fight. Although the assault on Fort Wagner was a costly failure, it proved to doubters the bravery of the black troops who unflinchingly threw themselves at a prepared position. The *Atlantic Monthly* attested, "Through the cannon smoke of that dark night the manhood of the colored race shines before many eyes that would not see."[13] The Confederacy reacted to the Union's black regiments by declaring that any black caught in uniform would be executed on the spot. Ironically, near the end of the war, the Southern government was so desperate for troops that it reluctantly authorized the formation of black units. The war ended, however, before any of these were mobilized.

Inconclusive Year

From early 1864 through the end of the war, the South was increasingly feeling the strain of war. Northern armies had swept through the western Confederacy, capturing strategically important cities, destroying railroads, and continually harassing the Southern armies. Few supplies were left. Southern combat uniforms, for example, could not be replaced, and troops appeared on the field in any clothing they could find, sometimes donning parts of Union uniforms when the need arose. Confederate armies were feeling the effects of scarcity, but so were the Southern citizens. High inflation made money nearly valueless in the South, and what food it could buy was running low. Jefferson Davis's government could do nothing to remedy the situation. Since the South feared a strong central government, Davis had little power and most legislation ended up in continual debate. The citizens and the armies remained ill clothed, underfed, and under the constant threat of attack.

Jefferson Davis

Despite the lack of supplies, Confederate morale was still good. The armies were willing to continue the fight even without shoes or food. But battlefield victory eluded the South. In May, Grant and Lee clashed in Virginia in a series of inconclusive battles. The engagements were costly for both sides; the North could recoup its losses, but the South could not. Lee, however, was keeping Grant at bay. Grant pressed toward Richmond but was stalled at every turn. Eventually Grant laid siege to Petersburg, Virginia, the vital rail junction that supplied Richmond. The siege lasted until the end of the war.

The March to Victory

While Grant campaigned against Richmond, Union armies under General William T. Sherman moved toward Atlanta. Opposing Sherman was Joseph E. Johnston and a force of sixty thousand Confederates. Sherman wanted to draw Johnston into a battle on open terrain, while Johnston kept to defensive positions. The two armies maneuvered without major confrontation. Jefferson Davis decided that Johnston's delaying tactics would not win the war. Davis replaced Johnston with John B. Hood, who launched attacks against Sherman. The strategy failed, and Hood retreated his men into Atlanta.

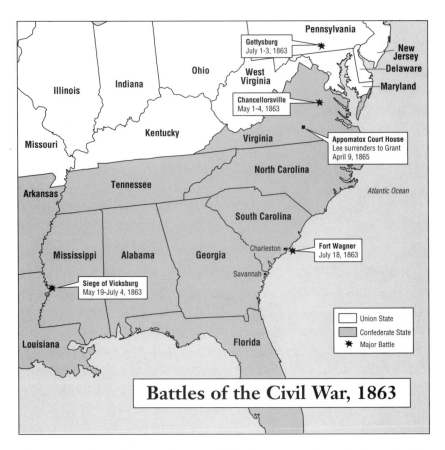

Battles of the Civil War, 1863

Sherman forced Hood out of Atlanta on September 1; the Union troops then set the city aflame. Hood's diminishing force moved north to Tennessee in a bold plan to draw Sherman away from the Deep South. But Sherman had his priorities. He dispatched a smaller force to tangle with Hood but committed the bulk of his army to a march through Georgia. Sherman's trek from Atlanta to the port city of Savannah was nearly unopposed. Along the way the Union army burned homes, pillaged livestock and private property, and tore up rail lines. Sherman's intention was to break the Southerners' will to fight and to destroy their ability to continue the war. The devastation was egregious. One Georgia native wrote,

> The dwellings that were standing all showed signs of pillage, and on every plantation we saw the charred re-

mains of the ginhouse and packing screw, while here and there lone chimney stacks, "Sherman's sentinals," told of homes laid in ashes. The infamous wretches! I couldn't wonder now that these poor people should want to put a rope around the neck of every red-handed "devil of them" they could lay their hands on.[14]

Southerners were bitter but helpless. On December 21 Sherman entered Savannah and offered the city to President Lincoln as a Christmas gift.

From Savannah, Sherman turned north and cut a path through South Carolina, the birthplace of secession. Charleston surrendered without a fight and was spared the wrath of the marauding Union troops. Sherman continued northward through North Carolina in an effort to link up with Grant in Virginia. In April 1865 Grant succeeded in seizing the rail lines that supplied Richmond. Lee was forced to evacuate the city. His army of barely fifty thousand men tried to move South to link up with other Confederate armies, but Grant, with a force more than twice that size, cut him off. Weighing the continued cost of fighting, Lee asked Grant for surrender terms. On April 9 the two generals met at Appomattox Court House in Virginia to arrange for the surrender. "Unconditional Surrender" Grant offered

After his forces were reduced to a mere fifty thousand men, General Lee decided to surrender. He and Union general Grant met at Appomattox Court House and signed a surrender that officially ended the war.

generous terms, and Lee accepted gratefully. Following Lee's lead, the other Confederate armies in the South surrendered in turn. By May all Southern troops had resigned to their fate: The war was over. America had lost more than six hundred thousand men in this, the nation's most costly fight.

Reconstruction

On April 14, five days after Lee's surrender, President Lincoln was assassinated. His successor, Andrew Johnson, was charged with the task of rebuilding the South in the war's aftermath. Before Johnson took office, there had been a plan for Reconstruction. In December 1863 Lincoln had foreseen the need for a

method of bringing Southern states back into the Union when the war ended. His idea was to offer a pardon to every Southerner who took an oath to uphold the Constitution. Furthermore, once 10 percent of a state's population had taken this oath, the repatriated Southerners could then begin forming a state government, provided they agreed that the new state constitution would ban slavery. Lincoln had always

Andrew Johnson

believed that his presidential duty was to preserve the Union, but many saw his Reconstruction plan as too lenient; staunch Republicans wanted the South to bear the punishment for the crime of secession.

Like Lincoln, Johnson wanted to reunite the nation as quickly as possible. Although he knew that punitive measures would only further divide the nation, Johnson also was given to a lenient policy because he was seeking voter support in the South for the next presidential election. Johnson borrowed part of Lincoln's plan. He offered a pardon to Southerners willing to take a loyalty oath, but he did not extend this privilege to officeholders in the Confederate government and military or to some well-known Southern aristocrats. He allowed for the election of state governments that were required to abolish slavery before they would be recognized. What Johnson failed to envision in his Reconstruction plans was the role that blacks were to play in rebuilding the South.

Two Opposing Plans

Although the Thirteenth Amendment, passed in 1865, guaranteed basic rights to the freed slaves, President Johnson was not interested in using federal authority to protect African Americans. Johnson was not in favor of black enfranchisement, and he was satisfied to let the states handle their own former-slave populations. "White men alone must manage the South,"[15] Johnson declared. Given such leeway, the Southern states passed laws that kept blacks out of government, tied to their plantation lifestyle, and subject to indiscriminate harassment. These black codes infuriated Northern Republicans, most of whom had been fighting for the abolitionist cause since before the war. The radical Republicans in Congress advocated immediately giving African Americans the vote, but the moderate Republicans agreed with Johnson that states would best deal with the problem. The moderates, however, did feel that blacks deserved more federal protection; thus, Congress passed the Civil Rights Act in 1866, which offered more legal rights to African Americans. Johnson vetoed the legislation, but Congress repassed the law over the president's veto.

President Johnson and the radical Republicans were also at odds on how best to carry out Reconstruction. Harvey Watterson, a Tennessee Unionist disillusioned with the president's plan, predicted, "A fight between the Radicals and the Executive is inevitable. Let it come. The sooner the better for the whole country."[16] In June 1866 Congress drafted the Fourteenth Amendment, which extended citizenship to all African Americans. Since no Southern states had yet to meet the requirements to rejoin the Union, Congress made the acceptance of the Fourteenth Amendment another stipulation of readmission. Johnson urged the Southern states to reject the amendment, and all but Tennessee did. The amendment would not gain enough state support to ratify it until 1868. Seeing Johnson as an obstacle, Congress chose to circumvent his authority and begin passing more radical legislation. Congress abolished the Southern governments set up under Johnson, and they proposed that new governments could only gain acceptance when they had registered all eligible black voters. To protect the blacks and make sure these Reconstruction acts were carried out, Congress stationed federal troops in the South. Johnson vetoed these measures, but the Republican Congress easily repassed them.

No End to Hostilities

Congress then passed other legislation aimed at curbing Johnson's power. The president violated one of these measures, and congressional leaders called for his removal from office. In February 1868 both houses of Congress voted to impeach the president. Johnson's absence, however, did not ensure that Reconstruction would progress smoothly. In 1869 the Fifteenth Amendment extended the right to vote to all citizens regardless of race, but the South used everything from poll taxes to intimidation to keep blacks from utilizing that privilege. White resistance did not die quickly. It was not until 1870 that all former Confederate states had been readmitted to the Union, but even an acceptance of the measures required for recognition by the central government did not mean that Reconstruction had succeeded. Bitterness against the North and the poor treatment of African Americans lasted into the twentieth century. The wounds that prompted separation and war had not healed.

---

1. Quoted in Geoffrey C. Ward with Ric Burns and Ken Burns, *The Civil War: An Illustrated History*. New York: Alfred A. Knopf, 1991, p. 12.

2. Quoted in Kenneth M. Stampp, ed., *The Causes of the Civil War*. Rev. ed. New York: Simon & Schuster, 1974, p. 27.

3. Quoted in Ward, *The Civil War*, p. 20.

4. Quoted in Milton Meltzer, ed., *Voices from the Civil War: A Documentary History of the Great American Conflict*. New York: Thomas Y. Crowell, 1989, p. 24.

5. Quoted in Mark E. Neely, Jr., *The Last Best Hope of Earth: Abraham Lincoln and the Promise of America*. Cambridge, MA: Harvard University Press, 1993, p. 63.

6. Quoted in Mario M. Cuomo and Harold Holzer, eds., *Lincoln on Democracy*. New York: A Cornelia & Michael Bessie Book, 1990, p. 204.

7. Quoted in Bruce Catton, *The Coming Fury*, vol. 1 of *The Centennial History of the Civil War*. Garden City, NY: Doubleday, 1961, p. 355.

8. Quoted in Meltzer, *Voices from the Civil War*, p. 48.

9. Quoted in Ward, *The Civil War*, p. 90.

10. Quoted in Ward, *The Civil War*, p. 167.

11. Quoted in Ward, *The Civil War*, p. 235.

12. Quoted in Meltzer, *Voices from the Civil War*, p. 104.

13. Quoted in James M. McPherson, *Battle Cry of Freedom: The Civil War Era*. New York: Ballantine Books, 1989, p. 686.

14. Quoted in Meltzer, *Voices from the Civil War*, p. 174.

15. Quoted in Eric Foner, *A Short History of Reconstruction, 1863–1877*. New York: Harper & Row, 1990, p. 84.

16. Quoted in Foner, *A Short History of Reconstruction*, p. 103.

CHAPTER 1

The Road to War

"The South is not seeking secession as much as it is being compelled to such action by a central government that has forsaken its republican principles."

Secession Is Justifiable

These days Northern congressmen would attest that their Southern brethren are advocating secession from the Union to purposefully provoke a conflict. To these gentlemen, secession is an act intended to bring an end to the republican principles on which this nation was founded. What these esteemed orators forget is that the South is not seeking secession as much as it is being compelled to such action by a central government that has forsaken its republican principles. Chief among these abandoned ideals is the right prescribed to each state to determine its own conduct, its own policies, its own future.

Free and Independent States

This is not a new philosophy sprung from the South's desire for autonomy; rather, it is one of the beliefs laid down by the founders of this nation. It is the language of the Declaration of Independence that proclaims that the collective states in this union

> are, and of right ought to be, free and independent states; and that, as free and independent states, they have full power to levy war, conclude peace, contract alliances, establish commerce, and to do all other acts and things which independent states may of right do.

As free and independent states, the members of this union have granted certain powers to a central government. But this central government was never granted the authority to abridge the rights of its member states.

Thus, the questions that come before this nation are: Has the central government in Washington overstepped its authority? and, Who has suffered because of such infractions? The answers to these questions are clear. The central government has ceased to be an administrative body reflecting the needs of the member states. It has become a tool of Northern interests intent on depriving the South of its economic institutions and its voice in matters of state. Observing the political leanings of the Congress, South Carolina senator John C. Calhoun has rightly deduced, "It is manifest, that on all questions between [the North] and the South, where there is a diversity of interests, the interest of the latter will be sacrificed to the former, however oppressive the effects may be."[1] Is this the type of state sovereignty sought by the nation's forefathers? No, this is the tyranny of a central government that has too easily been manipulated by the opinions of only half the nation.

The Challenge to State Sovereignty

State sovereignty is one of the cornerstones of this country. Currently, however, this notion seems to be the subject of debate. Or more precisely, state sovereignty is being challenged by Northerners who have a specific objective in mind: the elimination of slavery. To any reasonable man, there should be no question that the states have the right to defend the institutions and lifestyles that their citizens desire. But Northern abolitionists have characterized the elimination of slavery as a moral crusade and, thus, are determined to procure the powers of the central government to eradicate what they see as a blight upon the nation. The decision to tolerate slavery, however, is a political and economic controversy—one that should be addressed by the people of individual states or territories and not one mandated by a biased central government.

The issue of slavery has divided the Union since our nation's inception, and only by legislative means has the balance of power between slaveholding states and free states been maintained. Ensuring this equilibrium was important because it meant that neither side would dominate in Congress nor in the electoral college, the body by which the nation's chief politician is determined. But that balance has been upset in recent years by laws designed to give the North more governmental influence. Where once the number of free and slave states stood evenly at fifteen apiece, the Compromise of 1850 has tipped the balance in favor of the North. With California's entry into the Union as a free state—in trade, not for the addition of a slave state but for a stricter policy of returning fugitive slaves caught in Northern states—Northern interests now hold the majority in governing the entire nation.

As if control of Congress was not enough, it appears from the election of Abraham Lincoln, a Republican with an abolitionist platform, that every level of government policy making will cater to Northern sympathies. There shall be no neutrality from a president elected because of his abolitionist agenda. As Senator Robert Toombs of Georgia has stated, "Surely no one will deny that the election of Lincoln is the endorsement of the policy of those who elected him, and an endorsement of his own opinions."[2] The South is powerless against a chief executive who will back a congress that favors abolition.

Abolition Is a Coercive Act

Without recourse to the government, what options does the South possess to stave off the forced emancipation of its slaves? The economy of the South is based on physical labor, an obligation that is borne out by the toil of whites and blacks. It is common knowledge that blacks compose a large percentage of the labor force in the South, and it would not be inappropriate to say that slavery drives the Southern economy. The South is devoid of the manufacturing base of the North. Even the shipping of Southern goods is controlled by Northern merchant fleets. Without the strength of slave hands, the economy of the South would be ruined. Is it reasonable to expect that the South would willingly relinquish its livelihood? The Constitution preserves the right to hold slaves, and Southerners are determined to protect their property.

The abolition of slavery is a coercive act meant to deprive the South of its economic power and set loose a large impoverished population on the entire region. And it will be foisted upon the people of the South by the government that is supposed to serve them. How can Southerners accept such governmental legislation, especially when their voice has been silenced in Congress? These aggressive policies to contain slavery and restrict the rights of slaveholding states have understandably fostered resentment in the South. And now there is nothing but a widespread feeling of agitation. Senator Calhoun warned a few years ago that this agitation has been growing for some time, and he rightly asked, "Is it, then, not certain, that if something is not done to arrest it, the South will be forced to choose between abolition and secession?"[3]

No Option but to Secede

Well, it is now the eleventh hour. Northern policymakers control the Congress, and an abolitionist is now waiting to assume the mantle of the nation's chief executive. It is only a matter of time before the Constitution that has protected the right to hold slaves as property will be cast aside by sectional interests bent on freeing the Negroes. But Southern patriots are not dormant. The legislature of South Carolina has already amended its state constitution to anticipate the fateful day when Mr. Lincoln takes his seat:

> The guarantees of the Constitution will then no longer exist; the equal rights of the States will be lost. The Slaveholding States will no longer have the power of self-government, or self-protection, and the Federal Government will have become their enemy."[4]

With the inevitable laid before them, Southerners will be forced to resurrect the principles on which this nation was founded and construct for themselves a confederacy wholly dissolved from the Union to the north.

1. Quoted in Kenneth M. Stampp, ed., *The Causes of the Civil War*. Rev. ed. New York: Simon & Schuster, 1974, p. 26.

2. Quoted in William Dudley, ed., *The Civil War: Opposing Viewpoints*. San Diego: Greenhaven Press, 1995, p. 91.

3. Quoted in Stampp, *The Causes of the Civil War*, p. 28.

4. Quoted in Henry Steele Commager, ed., *The Blue and the Gray: The Story of the Civil War as Told by Participants*. New York: Bobbs-Merrill, 1950, p. 7.

"To believe that a state has the right to dissolve the Union is to acknowledge the ineffectual nature of government and to invite anarchy."

Secession Is Not Justified

The United States of America is, as its name attests, a union of states. The nation is bound by a constitution that the states have agreed to uphold. The representatives of the people in each state have pledged to defend the Constitution and to preserve its principles of unity. Yet there now exists a belief in many Southern states that this Union can be dissolved, that these states can voluntarily withdraw from their compact to act as one nation. But examination of the Constitution, the contract that binds the states, reveals that the notion that states can willfully secede from the Union is misguided in origin and illegal in execution.

The Purpose of the Constitution

The Constitution of the United States was drafted in 1787 because the country was then a confederacy of independent states that lacked internal cohesion. Without a strong central government, the states conducted their affairs independently. They printed their own currency, they imposed tariffs against each other, they raised armies on their own, and they made international agreements to benefit themselves; in essence, they were not united, they were not a nation.

The ratifying of the U.S. Constitution was a testimony to the will of a people who desired to make this conglomeration into a nation that could act as one. That constitution has been a source of pride to this country for nearly a century.

Secession Is Treason

To sever the sacred contract that was devised by all to protect and govern all is an act of treason. Treason is the true name of the secessionist cause in the South. Southern statesmen now wish to renege on their solemn pledge to defend the Constitution. Southern constituencies now wish to secede from the Union to which they as citizens swore allegiance. Such actions are plainly illegal, and to insist that some citizens are above the laws that bind others is to defile the principles on which the Union was founded.

By ratifying the Constitution and joining the Union, all states gave up their powers to govern themselves as independent nations. They surrendered their autonomy to the government of the United States in order to form a more perfect union. Furthermore, the Union thus formed was not conceived of as being a temporary alliance; the nature of the Union was permanent. Even as Southern states declared their secession, the new president, Abraham Lincoln, maintained in his inaugural speech,

> Perpetuity is implied, if not expressed, in the fundamental law of all national governments. It is safe to assert that no government proper ever had a provision in its organic law for its own termination.[1]

States Cannot Resign from the Union

President Lincoln has resolved, neither as a Northerner nor as a Republican but as an elected official of the United States and as a defender of its founding precepts, to deny any state or confederation of states the power to secede from the Union. He has rightly concluded that states cannot by will or force absolve themselves from the contract to maintain the Union. In the president's words,

> No state, upon its own mere motion, can lawfully get out of the Union,—that *resolves* and *ordinances* to that effect are legally void; and that acts of violence within any state or states against the authority of the United States are insurrectionary or revolutionary, according to circumstances.[2]

To believe that a state has the right to dissolve the Union is to acknowledge the ineffectual nature of government and to invite anarchy. This constitutional government is run by the voting public, who make their desires known by the way they cast their ballots. That is the essence of democracy; the majority opinion directs the course of the nation. As the *Cincinnati Daily Commercial* concludes, "If any minority have the right to break up the Government at pleasure, because they have not had their way, there is an end of all government."[3] Clearly the Southerners represent the minority opinion on many issues. The election of Abraham Lincoln over Southern candidate John C. Breckinridge shows that Southern political views lack the support of the citizen majority. The resistance to extending slavery into new territories indicates the prevailing attitude against the spread of that institution. And the dominating sentiment in Congress toward maintaining a strong central government confounds the notion that individual states have the power to override the laws of the nation. Because the nation's policies do not favor the South's cause in these matters, Southerners have decided that government may be freely dissolved.

Southern Demands Are Undemocratic

This petulance insults the democratic spirit of this country. These secessionists would have the American public believe that the democratic process is designed to deprive the South of its rights and liberties. Has not the government already shown itself willing to protect the rights of Southerners many times in the past? Congress has made no moves to abolish the institution of slavery in the South. It has made compromises that allowed free states into the Union only when a like number of slave states were admitted. It has even implemented the Fugitive Slave Law to help ensure that slaves will be returned to their plantations if they are caught fleeing into free states.

Congress has effected this legislation and yet Southerners are still not content because they fear that these policies may change. Well, policies may change if it is the will of the people of this nation. But that is the spirit of republican government.

These secessionists claim that they wish to establish their own free government. But how strong can that government be if it has been created by turning its back on democracy? There would be nothing to prevent states from seceding when they feel they have been treated unfairly. Such a government is a sham.

True Patriots Will Defend the Union

A nation must be strong. It must be willing to defend itself against efforts to disrupt its unity. It must acknowledge the will of the people as its guiding force. This government, this union, must preserve those ideals because the alternative will destroy the freedoms and privileges that so many Americans hold dear. As the *Chicago Journal* has rightly assessed,

> Without a Union that is *free*, without a Constitution that can be enforced, without an authority to command respect and obedience, without acknowledged deference to the voice of the people, in its constitutional majority, which cannot be arrogantly and safely violated or despised, our Republic ceases to be a Government, our freedom will be quickly supplanted by anarchy and despotism, and all the cherished hopes of our country and mankind, for enduring, and national freedom, will be blasted.[4]

The duty of all patriotic Americans is to defend the Union, to preserve the democratic principles that give the people a voice in government, to prove that self-rule works and is a desirable form of government for all free men. For if this country does not stand beside its republican beliefs, it will cease to be a nation. The Constitution will be mocked by monarchs and despots who would choose to keep those yearning for freedom in the iron grip of tyranny. Americans will no longer hold that unique place as exemplars of liberty and self-rule; in the eyes of the world they will cease to be Americans.

1.   Quoted in Mario M. Cuomo and Harold Holzer, eds., *Lincoln on Democracy*. New York: A Cornelia & Michael Bessie Book, 1990, p. 203.

2.   Quoted in Cuomo and Holzer, *Lincoln on Democracy*, p. 204.

3.   Quoted in James M. McPherson, *Battle Cry of Freedom: The Civil War Era*. New York: Ballatine Books, 1989, p. 247.

4.   Quoted in Kenneth M. Stampp, ed., *The Causes of the Civil War*. Rev. ed. New York: Simon & Schuster, 1974, p. 146.

"It is a paradoxical state of things to see a country which boasts of its freedom, nursing and sustaining the most odious system of slavery known on earth."

Slavery Must Be Abolished

There is no greater evil nor greater wrong than the enslavement of another person. Chattel slavery, the holding of people as property, violates the laws of both God and man and stands as a terrible disgrace upon this land. Few have stated this point more clearly than the noted abolitionist editor William Lloyd Garrison: "The one great, distinctive, all-conquering sin in America, is its system of chattel slavery."[1]

A Sin Against God

It is all the more troubling to find that those who urge a continuation of this vile institution seek justification for it in religious and natural law. The proposition that God created one race so inferior in all respects to any other, with no purpose other than subservience to a master, insults the Almighty and twists the teachings of Christianity. For it is clear that God intended that all men, as the sons of Adam, enjoy an equal right to liberty. In their zeal to find support for the peculiar and indefensible institution of slavery, its proponents conveniently ignore God's warning against the buying and selling of another person. In the Bible, God makes his views on this matter known when he states, "He that Stealeth a Man, and

41

Selleth him, or if he be found in his Hand, he shall surely be put to Death."

To buy and sell another human being, to separate mothers from children and husbands from wives, to subject a man or woman to continual hard labor and to the other cruel punishments of slavery, is to sin against God. This should be clear to all. But if it is not, one need only read the words of former slaves to comprehend the terrible wrongs of slavery. One former slave, for example, has described the tearing apart of families. "Babies was snatched from their mother's breast and sold. . . . Chilrens was separated from sisters and brothers and never saw each other agin. Course they cried. You think they not cry when they was sold like cattle?"[2]

Another former slave, Henry Bibb, recalls in a letter to his former master the brutal treatment inflicted on his wife and baby.

> To be compelled to stand by and see you whip and slash my wife without mercy, when I could afford her

Southern cruelty towards slaves compelled many Northerners to join abolitionist groups.

no protection, not even by offering myself to suffer the lash in her place, was more than I felt it to be the duty of a slave husband to endure. . . . My infant child was also frequently flogged by Mrs. Gatewood, for crying, until its skin was bruised literally purple.[3]

Such is the cruel existence of the black slave in these United States. None but the most callous of spirit could fail to be moved by such woeful tales. And yet there are many who argue for slavery's preservation.

"All Men Are Created Equal"

To those misguided souls, we offer additional support for the abolitionist cause, this time to be found in the origins of this proud nation. The nation's founders waged a righteous and bloody war in their determination to live as free men. The principles that guided their actions have as much meaning today as they did during America's War of Independence. The American Anti-Slavery Society, founded in Philadelphia in December 1833, reminds us of those essential principles in its "Declaration of Sentiments." This declaration states that

> more than fifty-seven years have elapsed since a band of patriots convened in this place to devise measures for the deliverance of this country from a foreign yoke. The cornerstone upon which they founded the TEMPLE OF FREEDOM was broadly this—"that all men are created equal; that they are endowed by their Creator with certain inalienable rights; that among these are life, LIBERTY, and the pursuit of happiness." At the sound of their trumpet-call, three millions of people rose up as from the sleep of death, and rushed to the strife of blood; deeming it more glorious to die instantly as freemen, then desirable to live one hour as slaves.[4]

That distinguished document that we call the Constitution of the United States has been interpreted by some as protecting and even encouraging the institution of slavery. But this is a false and dangerous interpretation. As the famed abolition-ist Frederick Douglass has said, this interpretation assumes that the Constitution "does not mean what it says, and that it says what it does not mean." Anyone who takes the trouble to read the Constitution will immediately ascertain its true meaning. As Douglass states,

> Its language is "we the people;" not we the white peo-ple, not even we the citizens, not we the privileged class, not we the high, not we the low, but we the peo-ple; not we the horses, sheep, and swine, and wheel-barrows, but we the people, we the human inhabitants; and, if negroes are people, they are included in the benefits for which the Constitution of America was or-dained and established.[5]

As Mr. Douglass points out, there can be no misunderstand-ing the Constitution's intent. To allow slavery to continue is to defile the admirable principles on which this nation was founded. To tolerate slavery is to weaken this nation's stand-ing in the eyes of the world.

Slavery Prevents Southern Progress

Though it is difficult to see how anyone could fail to be swayed by the moral, political, and legal considerations that favor abolition, a practical argument can also be made. Slav-ery continues to the detriment of Southern progress. While Northern cities experience growth in population and advances in manufacturing, transportation, and public services, the South remains mired in backwardness. In that unhappy land of so-called Southern gentility, a privileged few enjoy great wealth while the masses live in hopeless poverty.

Slavery is the root of this problem. Southerners have grown comfortable—some would say lazy—with their system of manual labor. While Southerners tend their fields and argue over the price of an ignorant slave at auction, Northerners

Many residents of the North felt that slavery created a system in which a privileged few controlled all of the Southern wealth.

build modern factories. While businesses in the North profit from the efficient labors of their workers, who are motivated by personal ambition and the promise of higher wages, Southern agriculture lumbers on with slaves whose only motivation is avoiding the master's lash. The free-labor practices of the North have created a healthy middle class that is poised to lead this nation toward the future while the slaveholding South lags behind with its two-class system of rich and poor.

Slavery, U.S. secretary of state William H. Seward once observed, has drained the South of its intelligence, vigor, and energy. After a trip through Virginia, he wrote of "an exhausted soil, old and decaying towns, wretchedly-neglected roads . . . absence of enterprise and improvement . . . such has been the effect of slavery."[6]

"The Most Odious System . . . on Earth"

Northerners are not alone in their observations of the South's lagging position or in their identification of slavery as the culprit. Hinton R. Helper, a well-respected writer who hails from the great state of South Carolina, bears no love for the Negro race. But he is a realist, and he minces no words when he writes of the economic disaster that slavery has brought to his beloved South. His own investigations show that

> the causes which have impeded the progress and pros-
> perity of the South, which have dwindled our com-
> merce, and other similar pursuits, into the most con-
> temptible insignificance; sunk a large majority of our
> people in galling poverty and ignorance . . . entailed
> upon us a humiliated dependence on the Free States;
> disgraced us in the recesses of our own souls, and
> brought us under reproach in the eyes of all civilized
> and enlightened nations—may all be traced to one
> common source, and there find solution in the most
> hateful and horrible word, that was ever incorporated
> into the vocabulary of human economy—*Slavery!*[7]

The South unquestionably suffers more ill effects from slavery than the North. But it can also be argued that a gangrenous infection in an arm or leg threatens the health of the body as a whole. So it is with the United States today. The Evansville, Indiana, *Journal* writes that "our country can never reach its full stature and importance so long as this baleful influence extends over it. It is a paradoxical state of things to see a country, which boasts of its freedom, nursing and sustaining the most odious system of slavery known on earth."[8]

Compromise Is Not an Option

The situation as it stands today is clearly intolerable. Slave states and free states cannot coexist or govern as equals. Compromise is not an option; there can be no compromise with slavery. As one Illinois lawyer writes, "Liberty and slavery—Civilization and barbarism are *absolute* antagonisms. One or the other must perish on this Continent."[9]

The course is clear. Slavery must be abolished.

1. Quoted in David Brion Davis, *Antebellum American Culture: An Interpretive Anthology.* University Park: Pennsylvania State University Press, 1997, p. 420.

2. Quoted in Geoffrey C. Ward with Ric Burns and Ken Burns, *The Civil War: An Illustrated History.* New York: Alfred A. Knopf, 1991, p. 10.

3. Quoted in John Hope Franklin and Alfred A. Moss Jr., *From Slavery to Freedom: A History of African Americans.* New York: Alfred A. Knopf, 1994, p. 144.

4. Quoted in Davis, *Antebellum American Culture*, p. 426.

5. Quoted in William Dudley, ed., *Slavery: Opposing Viewpoints.* San Diego: Greenhaven Press, 1992, pp. 223–24.

6. Quoted in James M. McPherson, *Ordeal by Fire: The Civil War and Reconstruction.* New York: Alfred A. Knopf, 1982, p. 44.

7. Quoted in William Dudley, ed., *The Civil War: Opposing Viewpoints.* San Diego: Greenhaven Press, 1995, p. 66.

8. Quoted in Kenneth M. Stampp, ed., *The Causes of the Civil War.* Rev. ed. New York: Simon & Schuster, 1974, p. 108.

9. Quoted in Stampp, *The Causes of the Civil War*, p. 106.

"In all social systems there must be a class to do the menial duties, to perform the drudgery of life. . . . Fortunately for the South, she found a race adapted to the purpose."

Slavery Must Be Preserved

Southern prosperity depends on agriculture, and agriculture relies on the labor of slaves. It is distressing to hear Northerners revile slavery as an abomination, especially when North and South alike benefit from the labor of the hardworking Southern farmers and planters. Between 1800 and 1860 alone, for example, America saw a huge jump in its cotton exports, which amounted to only $5 million in 1800 but $191 million in 1860. Meeting the growing demand for cotton, sugar, tobacco, and other crops has not always been easy, but the South has accomplished this by making use of slaves who are well-suited for such labor.

An Invitation to Southern Ruin

Those in the North who now demand an end to slavery invite the absolute ruin of the Southern economy. Without slaves, writes University of Virginia mathematics professor Albert Taylor Bledsoe,

> Our lands . . . would become almost valueless for the want of laborers to cultivate them. The most beautiful garden-spots of the sunny South would, in the course

of a few years, be turned into a jungle, with only here and there a forlorn plantation. Poverty and distress, bankruptcy and ruin, would everywhere be seen.[1]

The freeing of 4 million Negro slaves would, in addition, destroy a cherished way of life. The polite, orderly, civilized society nurtured by generations of Southerners would suddenly have forced on it a huge population unused to caring for itself in any meaningful way. Social ruin would closely follow economic decline. This is evident in the comments of the esteemed senator from Maryland, Robert Goodloe Harper. No supporter of slavery, Mr. Harper nevertheless advocates the return of black slaves to Africa rather than allowing them to remain on American soil once they are freed.

> You may manumit [free] the slave, but you cannot make him a white man; he still remains a negro or mulatto. . . . He looks forward to no distinction, aims at no excellence, and makes no effort beyond the supply of his daily wants. . . . The authority of the master being removed, and its place not being supplied by moral restraints or incitements, he lives in idleness, and probably in vice, and obtains a precarious support by begging or theft.[2]

The senator's comments make clear the catastrophe that would befall Southern society should so many black slaves be freed. Mr. Harper is not alone in expressing distaste for the institution of slavery while at the same time admitting the terrible consequences that await Southerners. For example, one prosperous Kentucky planter known for his abolitionist leanings opposes the freeing of his own slaves in America because "they could never be equal to the Whites, either socially or intellectually, and that consequently friction, if not disaster, would result."[3]

A Positive Good

Unlike Mr. Harper and the Kentucky planter, many abolitionists fondly portray Negroes as human beings like ourselves;

however, the fact remains that blacks and whites are not the same. The black race are like children—they require the stern hand of a caring and authoritative parent. Absent constant vigilance in this regard, they will revert to a natural tendency toward insolence, idleness, and deceit.

This reality should not be portrayed as hateful or spiteful, just as slavery should not be depicted as immoral or evil. What is clear to those who are well-schooled in God's laws and the laws of nature is that the institution of slavery befits both. In the Bible, for example, the apostle Paul urges slaves to obey their masters and advises an escaped slave to return to his master. Likewise, natural law—which refers to whatever brings the greatest happiness to the whole—supports slavery because that institution clearly benefits society at large.

Far from being evil, slavery represents a positive good not only for society but for the black race as well. Senator Jefferson Davis of Mississippi, speaking to the Confederate Congress, expressed this point clearer than most: "In moral and social condition [African slaves] had been elevated from brutal savages into docile, intelligent, and civilized agricultural laborers, and supplied not only with bodily comforts but with careful religious instruction."[4]

The lessons of history can be equally instructive in the debate over preserving slavery. It is well known that all great societies have relied at one time or another on slavery or serfdom. Examples can be found in ancient Egypt, biblical Israel, Greece, Rome, France during the time of Charlemagne, and England at the time of the Magna Carta. As Senator R.M.T. Hunter of Virginia points out, "There is not a respectable system of civilization known to history whose foundations were not laid in the institution of domestic slavery."[5]

Falsity in the North

Although Northern abolitionists often explain their efforts to free Southern slaves as growing out of a humanitarian concern for the welfare of slaves, nothing could be farther from the truth. We all know that free blacks in the North have little freedom. Indeed, four Northern states—Ohio, Indiana, Oregon, and Mr. Lincoln's own home state of Illinois—have laws that discourage or even prohibit blacks from settling within their borders.

If concern for the black race's welfare were truly the motivation behind efforts to end slavery, then Northern abolitionists would first look closer to home. If they were to do so, they would find squalid poverty and wretchedness all around them. The Negro who works in a Northern factory is little more than a wage slave. But unlike our Negroes, who are at least assured long-term employment, medical care, and a place to live into old age, Negroes in the North are routinely subjected to job losses and wage cuts, and those who are cast out must starve or depend on the charity of others. Senator James Henry Hammond of South Carolina aptly contrasts Northern and Southern attitudes toward the black population:

> In all social systems there must be a class to do the menial duties, to perform the drudgery of life. . . . Fortunately, for the South she found a race adapted to the purpose. . . . The difference between us is that our slaves are hired for life and well-compensated. Yours are hired by the day, not cared for, and scantily compensated."[6]

Control Is the Real Issue

The Northern obsession with abolishing slavery emanates not from concern over the black race but from a desire to control the South. The North has on many occasions made clear its real intentions. Numerous tariffs and federal subsidies have been sought and adopted with the aim of protecting Northern business interests, from shipping and manufacturing to fishing and coal mines. Clearly, the North is bent on using the powers of the federal government of all the people to achieve its own ends. Those ends include absolute control over the government and the ultimate destruction of the South. Few have

understood this better than Senator Jefferson Davis. Address-
ing the Northerners in a speech before Congress, Senator
Davis described efforts to limit slavery in the new territories:

It is not humanity that influences you. It is that you
may have an opportunity of cheating us that you want
to limit slave territory. . . . It is that you may have a majority in the Congress of the United States and convert
the Government into an engine of Northern aggran-
dizement. . . . You want by an unjust system of legislation to promote the industry of the United States at
the expense of the people of the South.[7]

The South will not be a party to its own destruction, nor
will it allow the North to determine its future. Slavery is a part
of the Southern way of life and it is a necessary component of
the Southern economy. It must be preserved.

1. Quoted in William Dudley, ed., *Slavery: Opposing Viewpoints*. San Diego: Greenhaven
    Press, 1992, p. 199.
2. Quoted in Dudley, *Slavery*, p. 183.
3. Quoted in Page Smith, *Trial by Fire*, vol. 5 of *A People's History of the Civil War and Re-
    construction*. New York: McGraw-Hill, 1982, p. 3.
4. Quoted in Kenneth M. Stampp, ed., *The Causes of the Civil War*. Rev. ed. New York: Si-
    mon & Schuster, 1974, p. 118.
5. Quoted in James M. McPherson, *Ordeal by Fire: The Civil War and Reconstruction*. New
    York: Alfred A. Knopf, 1982, p. 45.
6. Quoted in Geoffrey C. Ward with Ric Burns and Ken Burns, *The Civil War: An Illus-
    trated History*. New York: Alfred A. Knopf, 1991, p. 17.
7. Quoted in William Dudley, ed., *The Civil War: Opposing Viewpoints*. San Diego: Green-
    haven Press, 1995, p. 17.

CHAPTER 2

A Nation at War

"Lincoln has crowned the pyramid of his infamies with an atrocity abhorred of men, and at which even demons should not suffer."

The Emancipation Proclamation Is a Travesty

The Emancipation Proclamation is a disaster for America. It does not, as supporters claim, place the North on some imagined moral high ground. Rather, it casts doubt on both the so-called wisdom of those who now stand at the nation's helm and on the president's sincerity about the reasons for fighting a war with the South. Over and over President Lincoln has said that his only goal in this war is to preserve the Union. Consider his remarks in a letter to the abolitionist New York *Tribune* editor Horace Greeley shortly before issuing a preliminary draft of the proclamation. In that letter, dated August 22, 1862, the president writes,

> My paramount object in this struggle *is* to save the Union, and is *not* either to save or to destroy slavery. If I could save the Union without freeing *any* slave I would do it, and if I could save the Union by freeing *all* the slaves I would do it; and if I could save it by freeing some and leaving others alone I would also do that. What I do about slavery, and the colored race, I do because I believe

it helps to save the Union; and what I forbear, I forbear because I do *not* believe it would help to save the Union.[1]

And yet, by abolishing slavery in the rebel states, as his proclamation does, all chance for compromise ends and with it goes any hope for reunion between North and South.

The seriousness of this blunder can be understood in the response from friends and foes. Southerners see Mr. Lincoln's proclamation as proof of their longheld suspicion that his aim in this war is not to preserve the Union but to usurp their constitutionally guaranteed right of self-determination. World leaders, whom the president had hoped to impress with this proclamation, have denounced it for its hypocrisy and for the violence it is likely to incite. Most troubling of all, loyal Northerners are incensed by the president's sudden switch from a goal of preserving the Union to that of freeing black slaves.

The Southern Response

The Southern response, predictable though it may be, is disturbing because it confirms the likelihood that reconciliation between North and South is impossible. Jefferson Davis, president

Abraham Lincoln's Emancipation Proclamation freed all slaves in Union-held territory. Southerners felt that the proclamation infringed upon their constitutional right of self-determination.

of the Confederacy, has described the Emancipation Proclamation as the "most execrable [detestable] measure recorded in the history of guilty man."[2]

Though chances of the South rejoining the North were already slim, thanks to Mr. Lincoln's proclamation, all hopes are dashed. In remarks to the Confederate Congress on January 12, 1863, Jefferson Davis states clearly that

> this proclamation will have another salutary effect in calming the fears of those who have constantly evinced the apprehension that this war might end by some reconstruction of the old Union or some renewal of close political relations with the United States. These fears have never been shared by me, nor have I ever been able to perceive on what basis they could rest. But the proclamation affords the fullest guarantee of the impossibility of such a result.[3]

Politicians (who, it may be argued, have a stake in fanning the flames of dissent), are not the only ones who are bitter toward the proclamation, its author, and the North.

Newspaper editorials have been equally severe in their assessment of the Emancipation Proclamation. The Richmond, Virginia, *Enquirer* has described it as the "last extremity of wickedness which it was left to our enemy to adopt." The newspaper goes on to say that the people of the North have long shown that they are

> of a character to destroy any possible remains of past sympathies, and to extinguish every pleasurable feeling with which we used to recall the brilliant events that occurred in the period of our association with them. . . . Lincoln has crowned the pyramid of his infamies with an atrocity abhorred of men, and at which even demons should suffer.[4]

As if this were not bad enough, the proclamation has also fostered criticism among those thought to be our friends abroad.

The Stinging Foreign Response

One of the main results Mr. Lincoln sought in declaring an end to slavery in the rebel states was European support for the Union or, failing that, a vow of neutrality in the war. The president, however, has been badly stung by the foreign response. Political leaders in Great Britain and France have exposed the proclamation as both a sham and a disgrace. As they astutely point out, Mr. Lincoln seems only too happy to free slaves in the rebel states (over which he has no control) while ignoring those slaves who toil in Union-friendly border states (where the rule of U.S. law still holds). As the London *Spectator* observes, "The principle asserted is not that a human being cannot justly own another, but that he cannot own him *unless he is loyal to the United States.*" [5]

Our European friends worry that the proclamation will prolong the war and incite blacks to attack whites despite language urging "the people so declared to be free to abstain from all violence." Their concerns may prompt them to throw their support behind the Confederacy, which would be a dire outcome for the Union cause.

The Loyal North

Perhaps most disturbing of all is the response among loyal Northerners—those whom the president, by law and by popular consent, represents. Many Americans who live in Northern or border states must now wonder about the cause for which they and their fathers, sons, and brothers have been dying. For some time now it has been portrayed to them that they fight and die to preserve the Union, and for this goal they were willing to put their lives on the line. Suddenly, however, Mr. Lincoln has shifted goals. The Emancipation Proclamation makes it all too clear that the aim of this war is not to preserve the Union but to end slavery. When the president issued his preliminary proclamation on September 22, 1862, says Ohio Democrat Clement L. Vallandigham, "War for the

Union was abandoned; war for the negro openly begun."[6]

And now the Union war effort faces possibly its gravest threat to date. Reports of desertions by Union soldiers are on the rise since the president signed the final proclamation on January 1, 1863. Newspapers have urged Union soldiers to desert as opposition to the proclamation grows in the loyal states of Michigan, Ohio, Iowa, Indiana, and Illinois. And soldiers are heeding this call. For example, the 128th Illinois recently lost all but thirty-five of its men thanks to the Emancipation Proclamation. And who can blame them? The salvation of the black man is not the cause for which they agreed to sacrifice their lives. As one midwestern father wrote to his soldier son, "I am sorry [that] you are engaged in this unholy, unconstitutional and hellish war . . . which has no other purpose but to free the negroes and enslave the whites. Come home. If you have to desert, you will be protected."[7]

The travesty that is the Emancipation Proclamation has been unmasked. It threatens not only to undo the gains that have been made but also assures the death of the United States. Thanks to Mr. Lincoln's Emancipation Proclamation, North and South will never again be one.

1. Quoted in Mario M. Cuomo and Harold Holzer, eds., *Lincoln on Democracy*. New York: A Cornelia & Michael Bessie Book, 1990, p. 253.

2. Quoted in Geoffrey C. Ward with Ric Burns and Ken Burns, *The Civil War: An Illustrated History*. New York: Alfred A. Knopf, 1991, p. 166.

3. Quoted in William Dudley, ed., *The Civil War: Opposing Viewpoints*. San Diego: Greenhaven Press, 1995, p. 191.

4. Quoted in John Hope Franklin, *The Emancipation Proclamation*. Garden City, NY: Doubleday, 1963, p. 68.

5. Quoted in Ward, *The Civil War*, p. 166.

6. Quoted in Dudley, *The Civil War*, p. 188.

7. Quoted in Ward, *The Civil War*, p. 187.

*"The Star Spangled Banner is now the harbinger of Liberty
and the millions in bondage . . . will rally under that banner
whenever they see it gloriously unfolded to the breeze."*

The Emancipation Proclamation Is a Righteous Act

The Emancipation Proclamation, signed by President Abraham Lincoln on January 1, 1863, accomplishes what no other document before it has done. By freeing the slaves in the rebellious states, the Emancipation Proclamation weakens the Confederacy and strengthens the Union—both at home and abroad. Most importantly, it assures that the Union will follow the path of righteousness in its cause against the rebel South.

The Moral High Ground

By his actions, the president has shown the world that the North—and the North alone—has chosen to take the moral high ground in this terrible war. He has once again demonstrated the courage and integrity for which he and the people of this nation are renowned. Upon hearing a preliminary draft of the proclamation at the September 22, 1862, meeting of the cabinet, Secretary of the Treasury Salmon P. Chase remarked that the proclamation represented the "dawn of a new era; and although the act was performed from an imperative sense of duty . . . it is nevertheless, though baptised in blood, an act of humanity and justice which the latest generation will cele-brate."[1]

In any endeavor of this magnitude, there always exists a po-tential for failure. No one is more aware of this potential—and of the terrible cost that failure would bring—than the presi-dent. Wars have been lost and elections squandered on far less serious grounds. But the president has courageously chosen to take the honorable road. As he stated in his annual message to Congress on December 1, 1862, only one month before the signing of the final Emancipation Proclamation, the nation's salvation lies on the path of honor, justice, and freedom for all.

> Fellow citizens, *we* cannot escape history. . . . The fiery trial through which we pass, will light us down, in honor or dishonor, to the latest generation. . . . The dogmas of the quiet past, are inadequate to the stormy present. . . . In *giving* freedom to the *slave*, we *assure* freedom to the *free*. . . . We must disenthrall [free] our-selves, and then we shall save our country.[2]

The path of righteousness, which would be justification enough, is not the sole reason for the president's actions. In issuing this proclamation, he has also sought to gain tactical advantage for the Union.

Putting Pressure on the South

Emancipation of the slaves is aimed at damaging the Southern economy and its military. Mr. Lincoln is said to harbor the view that Southern slaves who hear the words "all persons held as slaves . . . shall be . . . forever free" in the Emancipation Procla-mation will abandon their masters and flee northward. Under the strain of lost slave labor, the Southern economy—and with it the Confederate army—will crumble. While this hoped for event has not yet come to pass, the South is clearly feeling the pressure of the president's bold move.

Evidence of its effect can be found in numerous places. For example, one South Carolina plantation owner, a Mr. Walter

Blake, is said to have lost three hundred slaves to the Union once word of the proclamation reached them. The plantation owners understand better than most how much the Southern economy—and the Southern war effort—will suffer as a result of the president's action. Try as they might, and many have tried mightily, the plantation owners cannot keep their slaves from hearing about or acting on the proclamation's promise. As one escaped slave recalls,

> We heard that Lincoln gonna turn [us] free. Ol' Missus say there wasn't nothin' to it. Then a Yankee soldier told someone . . . that Lincoln done signed the 'Mancipation. Was wintertime and mighty cold that night, but everybody commenced getting ready to leave. Didn't care nothin' 'bout Missus—was going to the Union lines.[3]

Upon reaching Union lines, black slaves who have claimed their right to freedom are taking up arms on behalf of the Union cause. This is an additional tactical benefit foreseen by the president.

An Infusion of Manpower

It is no secret that the proud men of the Union army are exhausted and ready for this war to end. With no immediate end in sight, however, an infusion of manpower will only strengthen the Union's hand on the battlefield. Secretary of War Edwin M. Stanton has long urged the emancipation and arming of slaves but has won little support for that position. The president himself has been among the doubters. Nevertheless, he has finally seen the wisdom of such action. "The colored population," the president writes, "is the great *available* and yet *unavailed* of, force for restoring the Union."[4]

The final proclamation reflects this view when it declares that all "persons of suitable condition, will be received into the armed service of the United States to garrison forts, positions, stations, and other places, and to man vessels of all sorts in said service." With these simple words, President Lincoln has made it possible for the Union army to expand its ranks of able-bodied men by the thousands. This is a significant achievement, and the Union will see its reward in the devotion of those freed black slaves who take up the cause.

As the esteemed black abolitionist Frederick Douglass states, "The Star Spangled Banner is now the harbinger of Liberty and the millions in bondage, inured to hardships, accustomed to toil, ready to suffer, ready to fight, to dare and to die, will rally under that banner whenever they see it gloriously unfolded to the breeze."[5]

European Support

Among the many benefits promised by the Emancipation Proclamation is a less obvious but no less important one. The major powers of Europe, including Great Britain and France, will be forced to hold back support for the Confederacy, offer

Lincoln recognized a major advantage of the Emancipation Proclamation. He reasoned that slaves would be willing to fight for their freedom, depriving the South of a larger army and at the same time increasing Union manpower.

it instead to the Union, or take no position at all. The reason for this is simple: These great European powers have never accepted slavery, and the Emancipation Proclamation clearly states for the first time that ending slavery is a central aim of the Union war effort.

Reaction from Europe has been mixed, but the overall goal is within reach. Neither England nor France appears willing to openly oppose a United States determined to abolish slavery. Hopeful signs have come from people such as the great and influential English philosopher John Stuart Mill: "The triumph of the Confederacy would be a victory of the powers of evil which would give courage to the enemies of progress and damp the spirits of friends all over the civilized world. [The American Civil War] is destined to be a turning point, for good or evil, of the course of human affairs."[6]

"Queen Among the Nations"

No one, not the president nor the most ardent abolitionist, truly believes that the South will willingly abide by the terms of the Emancipation Proclamation. Sadly, the slavery debate will be settled only by more war. In the process, however, the North has shown that it will not abandon what it knows to be right and good.

The Emancipation Proclamation is a righteous act. Its enactment assures that a Union victory will be a victory for all Americans and that it will be viewed as such by all the civilized nations of the world. As Frederick Douglass writes, "The rebellion suppressed, slavery abolished, and America will, higher than ever, sit as a queen among the nations of the earth."[7]

1. Quoted in John Hope Franklin, *The Emancipation Proclamation*. Garden City, NY: Doubleday, 1963, p. 59.
2. Quoted in James M. McPherson, *Battle Cry of Freedom: The Civil War Era*. New York: Ballantine Books, 1989, p. 563.

3. Quoted in Geoffrey C. Ward with Ric Burns and Ken Burns, *The Civil War: An Illustrated History*. New York: Alfred A. Knopf, 1991, p. 177.

4. Quoted in Mark E. Neely Jr., *The Last Best Hope of Earth: Abraham Lincoln and the Promise of America*. Cambridge, MA: Harvard University Press, 1993, p. 118.

5. Quoted in William Dudley, ed., *The Civil War: Opposing Viewpoints*. San Diego: Greenhaven Press, 1995, p. 186.

6. Quoted in Ward, *The Civil War*, p. 167.

7. Quoted in Dudley, *The Civil War*, p. 186.

"The idea that all the constitutional guarantees of personal liberty are suspended . . . subjects the life, liberty and property of every citizen to the mere will of a military commander."

The President Does Not Have a Right to Suspend Civil Liberties During War

The war that now rages between North and South has taken its toll on all Americans, but possibly no one feels the weight of it more than the president. As commander in chief, he must daily make decisions that determine the fate of thousands of individuals as well as the nation's future. Decisions of this magnitude represent a huge responsibility, but the strain of even these events does not entitle the president to exceed his legal powers or to justify the suspension of constitutionally guaranteed freedoms.

To the contrary, the Constitution ensures that certain freedoms and rights exist regardless of who holds power or what events transpire. President Lincoln has clearly lost sight of this. His actions in recent months represent a striking abuse of the powers of his office and a disturbing assault on the constitutional rights of all Americans.

An Arrogant Assault on Democracy

From the moment the Confederates fired on Fort Sumter in April 1861, Mr. Lincoln has demonstrated a strikingly broad interpretation of the president's wartime powers. The list of questionable actions undertaken by him on "military grounds" is long and troubling. Over these past months he has waged war without congressional approval; seized Northern telegraph offices (under the pretext of preventing the transmission of subversive information); suspended the writ of habeas corpus, which prevents wrongful or unjustifiable detention; and proclaimed martial law, allowing civilians to be tried by military courts.

President Lincoln justifies these and other actions with sweeping statements such as this one: "I conceive that I may in an emergency do things on military grounds which cannot be done constitutionally by Congress."[1]

This thinking represents the height of arrogance. It constitutes an assault on all that Americans hold dear, as one group of Ohio Democrats points out in a letter to the president dated June 26, 1863:

> The idea that all the constitutional guarantees of personal liberty are suspended throughout the country at a time of insurrection or invasion in any part of it, places us upon a sea of uncertainty, and subjects the life, liberty and property of every citizen to the mere will of a military commander, or what he may say he considers the public safety requires.[2]

The president has clearly exceeded the bounds of his office as defined by the Constitution.

Suspension of the Writ of Habeas Corpus

This fact is most apparent in his decision to suspend the privilege of the writ of habeas corpus and declare martial law across all the United States. Suspension of the writ allows the arrest and detention not only of rebels, insurgents, and those who try to interfere with military enlistments or the draft but also of a broad and rather vague category that includes "all persons . . . guilty of any disloyal practice."[3] The declaration of martial law means that anyone accused of such crimes shall be tried by military rather than civilian courts, which represents another affront to the Constitution.

Mr. Lincoln first set out on this dangerous course about two weeks after the April 13, 1861, fall of Fort Sumter to Confederate troops. On April 27 he suspended the writ "at any point on or in the vicinity of the military line . . . between the City of Philadelphia and the City of Washington."[4] No doubt, his intention at this point was to keep the route to the nation's capital open should military reinforcements be needed. However, Mr. Lincoln went far beyond what might have been construed as "military necessity" when he suspended the writ and declared martial law across the entire United States on September 24, 1862.

In the many months following these actions by the president, tens of thousands of civilians—some say upwards of thirteen thousand—suspected of some vague form of disloyalty have been arrested by the military and detained without charges or trial. Those arrested under Mr. Lincoln's edicts include men whose only crimes were publicly (and usually drunkenly) shouting support for the Confederacy or omitting the traditional prayer for the president during church services.

While no patriotic American quarrels with the arrest of enemy agents and saboteurs or the military trials of guerillas and spies in active war zones, the arbitrary arrest of loyal Northerners and the substitution of military commissions for civilian courts is unacceptable. "This new doctrine," the respected New York Democrat Horatio Seymour has said, shows "that the loyal North lost their constitutional rights when the South rebelled."[5]

Disagreement Does Not Equal Disloyalty

In his zeal to root out those who might pose a real threat to the Union, Mr. Lincoln has confused disagreement with disloyalty. As a result, Northerners have witnessed a steady erosion of their constitutionally guaranteed right to freedom of speech. Among those who have felt the wrath of Mr. Lincoln's policies are newspaper editors, public officials, and other persons who publicly oppose the president's stance on the war.

One of the most well known of these cases involves Clement L. Vallandigham, a Democratic representative from Ohio. Mr. Vallandigham has openly opposed the president's war policies many times and in many different settings, including on the floor of the House of Representatives. In one speech to House members, Mr. Vallandigham likened arrests made under the Lincoln administration to the religious persecution of another era.

> Some two hundred years ago, men were burned at the stake, subjected to the horrors of the Inquisition, to all the tortures that the devilish ingenuity of man could invent—for what? For opinions on questions of religion. . . . And now, today, for the opinions on questions political, under a free government, in a country whose liberties were purchased by our fathers by seven years' outpouring of blood, and expenditure of treasure—we have lived to see men, the born heirs of this precious inheritance, subjected to arrest and cruel punishment at the caprice of a President.[6]

Not surprisingly, such strident accusations have attracted attention. This may explain the administration's response to a later speech given by Mr. Vallandigham on May 1, 1863, when he publicly accused the president of unnecessarily prolonging the war.

That same night a Union commander arrested and jailed Mr. Vallandigham. The next day a military commission convicted him of treason for uttering statements deemed disloyal and disruptive to the Union. In fact, Mr. Vallandigham was only expressing his concern for the Union and for upholding the sanctity of the Constitution. Members of the Ohio Democratic Convention sought to explain this in a letter to the president dated June 26, 1863:

> Mr. Vallandigham may differ with the President, and even with some of his own political party, as to the true

and most effectual means of maintaining the Constitution and restoring the Union; but this difference of opinion does not prove him to be unfaithful to his duties as an American citizen.[7]

Their appeal for a reversal of Vallandigham's conviction and sentence has fallen on deaf ears. But others have also tried to show the president the error of his ways, including members of his own political party.

Republican Criticism

Among Republican members of Congress who have registered their concerns are Lyman Trumbull, the senior senator from Mr. Lincoln's home state of Illinois; John P. Hale of New Hampshire; and William Pit Fesenden of Maine. Horace Greeley, the abolitionist editor of the New York *Tribune* and a Republican faithful, has on many occasions complained about military arrests of civilians. In one editorial written in August 1862, Greeley wrote,

In our poor judgment, nine-tenths of the arbitrary arrests thus far had far better not been made; but we would not deprive the government of the power to make them in a crisis like the present. Let it be distinctly understood, however, that each arrest will be made the subject of rigorous and dispassionate inquiry after peace, and that, while no one should suffer for his innocent mistakes in honestly endeavoring to serve his country, it will go very hard with any one who is proved to have gratified his own

Horace Greeley

malice or his love of exercising despotic power, without the warrant of public necessity.[8]

An Extraordinary Abuse of Power

While much about this war may be cause for debate, on the matter of presidential abuse of power the evidence is overwhelming. The president has gone too far. Despite his contention that he has acted in the nation's best interests, in truth his actions since the start of war represent an extraordinary abuse of power.

1. Quoted in James M. McPherson, *Ordeal by Fire: The Civil War and Reconstruction.* New York: Alfred A. Knopf, 1982, p. 263.
2. Quoted in William Dudley, ed., *The Civil War: Opposing Viewpoints.* San Diego: Greenhaven Press, 1995, p. 199.
3. Quoted in Mario M. Cuomo and Harold Holzer, eds., *Lincoln on Democracy.* New York: A Cornelia & Michael Bessie Book, 1990, p. 261.
4. Quoted in Geoffrey Ward with Ric Burns and Ken Burns, *The Civil War: An Illustrated History.* New York: Alfred A. Knopf, 1991, p. 61.
5. Quoted in Mark E. Neely Jr., *The Fate of Liberty: Abraham Lincoln and Civil Liberties.* New York: Oxford University Press, 1991, p. 193.
6. Quoted in Jeffrey Rogers Hummel, *Emancipating Slaves, Enslaving Free Men: A History of the American Civil War.* Chicago: Open Court, 1996, p. 257.
7. Quoted in Dudley, *The Civil War,* p. 196.
8. Quoted in Neely, *The Fate of Liberty,* p. 191.

"Must I shoot a simple-minded soldier boy who deserts, while I must not touch a hair of a wiley agitator who induces him to desert?"

The President Has a Right to Suspend Civil Liberties During War

From his first days in office, President Abraham Lincoln's primary goal has been the preservation of the Union. And now, as he tries to carry out this most difficult task, he is accused of abusing the powers of his office and of violating the constitutional rights of Americans. These accusations are baseless. They spring from political opponents—primarily Democrats—who seek to weaken the Republican president by maligning his reputation.

Unlike his critics, the president clearly understands his duty, which is to win this war. He also understands, better than most, that the Constitution empowers him—both as president and as commander in chief—to take extraordinary measures (if needed) to achieve that goal.

Over the last months the president has been forced to act in ways that no one would have envisioned if the nation were now at peace. Among the most often cited "abuses" is his decision to suspend the privilege of the writ of habeas corpus, which seeks to prevent wrongful or unjustifiable detention, and his proclamation of martial law, allowing civilians to be tried by military courts.

The Growing Peril

The decision to suspend the writ and declare martial law was not taken lightly. President Lincoln's first action in this regard came shortly after the disastrous April 13, 1861, Union surrender of Fort Sumter. At that time, emotions ran high and the president (and many other citizens) feared for the safety of the nation's capital. Their fear was well-founded, as a mob demonstrated on April 19 in Baltimore, Maryland, when it blocked the passage of Massachusetts troops assigned to guard Washington, D.C. That same night local authorities in Baltimore cut off access to the capital by burning strategic railroad bridges. In addition, the president had received reports that the Maryland legislature was planning a vote on secession. Had Maryland decided to secede, Washington, D.C. would have been cut off from the Union and in great peril. Though the latter did not come to pass, concern remained high for the nation's capital.

Union legislators and others bombarded Mr. Lincoln with dire warnings and urgent suggestions. For example, Orville Hickman Browning, a moderate Illinois Republican and a friend of the president's, warned Mr. Lincoln on April 22 that disaster awaited if Washington fell. "Communication ought to and must be kept open to Washington. Baltimore must not stand in the way. It should be seized and garrisoned, or, if necessary to the success of our glorious cause, laid in ruin."[1]

After much deliberation, the president undertook a much less severe, though no less serious, course of action. On April 27, 1861, President Lincoln suspended the writ of habeas corpus and declared martial law in the border states and along the route to the capital. Seventeen months later, on September 24, 1862, the president expanded both actions to cover the entire United States.

Sound Reasoning

His reasoning for these measures is sound, and his actions fall well within the bounds of the Constitution. The wanton destruction of public property and vocal calls for secession and resistance to the draft have spread throughout the North, threatening the stability of the Union and its ability to defend itself. As Mr. Lincoln has said on at least one occasion that he fears "'the fire in the rear'—meaning the Democracy, especially at the Northwest—more than our military chances."[2]

Civilian law enforcement and civilian courts, already busy before the war, cannot handle the many new threats to national security and public safety. Army officers must be free to arrest and detain all suspected traitors. It is for these reasons that the president has suspended the writ and proclaimed martial law. The language of the Constitution expressly permits this: "The Privilege of the Writ of Habeas Corpus shall not be suspended, unless when in Cases of Rebellion or Invasion, the public Safety may require it."

Can there be any doubt that the United States is now enmeshed in a rebellion of unprecedented proportions and that the public safety is threatened by Northerners who sympathize with the enemy? Under these extraordinary circumstances, Mr. Lincoln's actions have been both proper and necessary. The president has explained his thinking on this subject, noting that

> the constitution is different, *in its application* in cases of Rebellion or Invasion, involving the Public Safety, from what it is in times of profound peace and public security; and this opinion I adhere to, simply because, by the constitution itself, things may be done in the one case which may not be done in the other.[3]

The arrest and detention of civilians in the North by military authorities must be viewed through the lens of the extraordinary events now gripping the nation.

A Clear Case of Treason

One of the most celebrated of these cases involves Clement L. Vallandigham, a Democratic representative from Ohio. Mr.

Democratic representative Clement L. Vallandigham, an open opponent of Lincoln and his policies, was convicted of treason for publicly urging Union troops to desert.

Vallandigham makes no effort to hide his dislike for the president and his policies. His public rantings against the president are legendary, especially on the floor of the House of Representatives, where he once likened Mr. Lincoln to those who carried out the murderous Inquisition of an earlier century. While Mr. Vallandigham's remarks are insulting, they were at least tolerable until May 1, 1863.

On that date Mr. Vallandigham crossed the line between dissent and treason by publicly urging Union soldiers to desert, by declaring the South invincible, and by warning New England residents that their support for the war would

lead western states to leave the Union and join the Confederacy. Mr. Vallandigham was promptly arrested, tried, and convicted of treason for making disloyal statements aimed at
"weakening the power of the Government [to put down] an
unlawful rebellion."[4]

Predictably, Mr. Vallandigham whines that the government's actions are an attempt to stifle dissent. In a letter to
supporters, he states,

> I am here in a military bastile for no other offence than
> my political opinions, and the defence of them and of the
> rights of the people, and of your constitutional liberties.
> Speeches made in the hearing of thousands of you in de-
> nunciation of the usurpations of power, infractions of the
> Constitution and laws, and of military despotism, were
> the sole cause of my arrest and imprisonment.[5]

Any fair-minded person can see that Mr. Vallandigham's statements represent not simply a defense of the Constitution, as
he pretends, but treason.

"To Silence the Agitator"

In times of war, statements such as these cannot be ignored.
The laws of this nation permit the severest penalty—death—
for a deserter from the army. But what of the man who en-
courages the soldier to desert? Shall he be absolved of all responsibility? As Mr. Lincoln has so ably put it, "Must I shoot
a simple-minded soldier boy who deserts, while I must not
touch a hair of a wiley agitator who induces him to desert? . . .
I think that, in such a case, to silence the agitator, and save the
boy, is not only constitutional, but, withal, a great mercy."[6]

In fact, most of the arrests have not involved political
speech or even the president's most vocal opponents in the
northwestern states, as those Democratic critics try to paint it.
The list of civilians arrested and detained without benefit of
the writ or civilian trial hail mainly from the border states
(where Southern sympathy is rife) and includes persons

caught running the Union blockade and engaging in guerilla warfare against the North.

Responding to Extraordinary Events

If anything, public debate has grown more strident as the war drags on. Democratic newspapers and politicians continue their relentless attack on the president and on the Union cause, as can be seen in this Wisconsin newspaper headline immediately following Mr. Lincoln's reelection in 1864:

> The Union of States is gone forever. The South never will be subjugated. A revolution, already rife in the North, will burst with bloody fury at no distant day. The Northwestern Confederacy will surely be established. The Northwestern Confederacy will join hands with the South.[7]

Clearly, the attacks on the president have no basis in fact. Rather, they stem solely from political extremists who can find no other recourse against the president and the dominant party than to besmirch the good name of Abraham Lincoln.

As all Americans must know, extraordinary events sometimes require an extraordinary response. President Lincoln's actions during this war have at no time exceeded his constitutional powers. Nor can they in any way be construed as an abuse of the office of the president.

1.   Quoted in Mark E. Neely Jr., *The Fate of Liberty: Abraham Lincoln and Civil Liberties.* New York: Oxford University Press, 1991, p. 6.

2.   Quoted in James M. McPherson, *Battle Cry of Freedom: The Civil War Era.* New York: Ballantine Books, 1989, p. 591.

3.   Quoted in William Dudley, ed., *The Civil War: Opposing Viewpoints.* San Diego: Greenhaven Press, 1995, p. 202.

4.   Quoted in Geoffrey C. Ward with Ric Burns and Ken Burns, *The Civil War: An Illustrated History.* New York: Alfred A. Knopf, 1991, p. 189.

5.   Quoted in Dudley, *The Civil War,* p. 198.

6.   Quoted in Neely, *The Fate of Liberty,* p. 68.

7.   Quoted in Mark E. Neely Jr., *The Last Best Hope of Earth: Abraham Lincoln and the Promise of America.* Cambridge, MA: Harvard University Press, 1993, p. 138.

"Like all soldiers, blacks have to earn the respect of their peers on the field of battle, but blacks should not have to earn the right to enlist for combat."

Black Soldiers Should Be Allowed to Fight

Many people in this nation oppose the participation of black soldiers in the fight to save the Union. They accept the stereotypes that blacks are shiftless and unable to learn or adhere to the regimen of military life. What these naysayers need, however, is to witness the African American in combat. In the terrible hand-to-hand fighting at Milliken's Bend or the courageous assaults at Port Hudson, the valor and pride with which these soldiers fight erases all doubts as to their effectiveness in the front lines. Black soldiers have earned the right to fight alongside their white comrades, yet they remain a resource that is underestimated and underused. This nation must rise above its prejudices and concentrate all its resources on victory. Expand the role of the black soldier and give him the opportunity to help bring this war to a speedy conclusion.

Asking Only for the Chance to Fight

African Americans have fought for this nation in the Revolutionary War and in the War of 1812; once again they desire only to show their patriotism during this time of crisis. They ask no special treatment as soldiers. Like all soldiers, blacks have to earn the respect of their peers on the field of battle, but blacks should not have to earn the right to enlist for combat. In July 1862 Congress passed a militia act that empowered the government to conscript able-bodied men for service in the army. Under the jurisdiction of this bill, the government was given the authority to draft "persons of African descent" for "any war service for which they may be found competent."[1] This included the use of blacks as soldiers. With this governmental sanction, training black regiments and moving them into combat roles should be assured, but it is not. Most black enlistees are given menial duties and serve as guards or supply handlers in baggage trains.

Praise for Black Troops

Such lackluster occupations are not for men who have been trained, like all soldiers, to engage the enemy. These are skilled and highly motivated fighters. Some of these men have escaped slavedom only to take up arms against it. They will fight with a desire that is not shared by their white comrades—the desire to destroy the very system that kept them in bondage for so long. The white officers who command the black regiments are the first to praise the special character of their troops. Thomas Wentworth Higginson, commander of the First South Carolina Volunteers, declared after seeing his men in battle,

> No officer in this regiment now doubts that the key to the successful prosecution of this war lies in the unlimited employment of black troops. Their superiority lies simply in the fact that they know the country, while white troops do not, and, moreover, they have peculiarities of temperament, position, and motive which belong to them alone. Instead of leaving their homes and families to fight they are fighting for their homes and families.[2]

Not only is the tenacity of the black soldier a credit to his character, it is also a credit to the war effort. When the all-black First South Carolina Volunteers were formed, they were ordered to gather supplies and to destroy enemy industry in Georgia. General Saxton comments on his raw recruits:

> Although scarcely one month since the organization . . . was completed . . . these untrained soldiers have cap- tured . . . an amount of property equal in value to the cost of the regiment for a year. They have driven back equal numbers of rebel troops . . . [and] destroyed the salt-works along the whole line of this coast.[3]

With a fighting spirit and proven effectiveness in combat, black soldiers should be given more combat roles. This nation has more than 180,000 black troops in arms; let them be put to action, let them fight and die with the dignity of soldiers.

Enlisting Despite Prejudice

And dignity is what these men have. Despite the opinions of both Northerners and Southerners, who say this is a white man's war, these black patriots have arisen. They are paid seven dollars per month, compared to the thirteen dollars earned by white soldiers; they are barred from officer status; and they know that in the hands of the enemy they will be brutalized; yet they enlist by the thousands. As an editorial in the *Afro-American*, a black publication, proclaims,

> *White Americans* remember! that we know that in go- ing to the field we will neither get bounty, or as much wages even as you will receive for the performance of the same duty;—that we are well aware of the fact that if captured we will be treated like wild beasts by our enemies;—that the avenue to honor and promotion is closed to us; but for these things we care not. We fight for God, liberty and country, not money.[4]

Such unequal treatment would tax the determination of any patriot, but black soldiers are still willing to die for the cause. The Fifty-fourth Massachusetts Volunteers even elected to fight without pay rather than accept their debased salary. "Three cheers for Massachusetts and seven dollars a month"[5] was their battle cry as they marched through Florida. To the Fifty-fourth and other black regiments, the chance to take up arms in defense of liberty and the Union is an honor for which there is no compensation but freedom.

A Larger Army Will Speed Victory

The North still struggles with maintaining a large army. The imposition of the draft has already demonstrated the need for recruits. Let the test for combat volunteers be not their skin color but their willingness to take up the fight for the Union. What army could not use one hundred thousand more skilled riflemen, artillerymen, or cavalrymen? Put as many guns against an enemy as you can and you cannot fail to overcome them; keep those guns in reserve and you must answer why you choose to prolong your war unnecessarily. As esteemed orator Frederick Douglass has said in reference to the foolishness of the North's resistance to employing all its resources, "Men in earnest don't fight with one hand, when they might fight with two."[6]

Frederick Douglass

The people of this nation want to see an end to the terrible bloodshed. The defenders of the Union want victory, and they want it now. The federal troops who have been fighting and dying will abide by anything that can shorten their tenure in the front lines. As one white soldier commented,

> After a man has fought two years he is willing that any thing shal[l] fight for the purpose of ending the war. We

have become to[o] familiar with hardships to refuse to see men fight merely because their color is black.[7]

Employing more black combat troops will hasten victory for the North. They will help bring an end to the hardships faced by the soldiers and citizens of this country. They will aid in restoring the Union that Americans of all races respect and commend.

1. Quoted in James M. McPherson, *Battle Cry of Freedom: The Civil War Era*. New York: Ballantine Books, 1989, p. 500.

2. Quoted in Page Smith, *Trial by Fire*, vol. 5 of *A People's History of the Civil War and Reconstruction*. New York: McGraw-Hill, 1982, p. 309.

3. Quoted in Hondon B. Hargrove, *Black Union Soldiers in the Civil War*. Jefferson, NC: McFarland, 1988, p. 50.

4. Quoted in Smith, *Trial by Fire*, p. 313.

5. Quoted in John Hope Franklin and Alfred A. Moss Jr., *From Slavery to Freedom: A History of African Americans*. New York: Alfred A. Knopf, 1994, p. 215.

6. Quoted in William Dudley, ed., *The Civil War: Opposing Viewpoints*. San Diego: Greenhaven Press, 1995, p. 213.

7. Quoted in James M. McPherson, *Drawn with the Sword: Reflections on the American Civil War*. New York: Oxford University Press, 1996, p. 90.

"Reconciliation cannot derive from turning slave against master. The aim of this war is to suppress rebellion, not to provide recompense to the Negro for years of enslavement."

Black Soldiers Should Not Be Allowed to Fight

The people of the North must make many concessions in order to ensure victory in this great conflict, but arming Negroes to fight is not one of them. To mobilize black troops for combat purposes is to debase the white soldier and make him feel as though his blood and sweat are not enough to defeat the rebellious South. Such a move could foster dissension in the Union ranks and threaten the effectiveness of the army. Governor David Tod of Ohio contends that "to enlist a Negro soldier would be to drive away every white man out of service."[1] Raising black regiments will be a clear signal to the citizenry as well as the military that this war is being pursued to put the Negro on equal footing with the white man, not to save the Union. To persist in such a course of action will risk losing the sympathy and motivation of Northerners and will sully the just cause for which they fight.

Appropriate Roles for Blacks

Advocating this position is not to imply that there is no place in the Union cause for the black man. The status of the Negro, however, is currently under debate. They are not full citizens, and white troops do not wish to see blacks don the

Union uniform when their citizenship is in question. The black volunteer, however, may support the cause by helping relieve the white soldier from noncombat duties. General Ulysses S. Grant has found appropriate jobs for the Negro volunteers under his command: "I am using them as teamsters, hospital attendants, company cooks and so forth, thus saving soldiers to carry the musket."[2] Black men may also help in the quartermaster corps, ensuring that the fighting troops are well supplied to pursue victory. There is no shame in such service; working in supply is a vital contribution to the war effort. And the public supports this type of recruitment. There are, however, few people in the North willing to entertain the notion of armed black servicemen.

Opposition from All Sides

Military men asked about the rationality of arming black soldiers are typically resolved against it. General William Tecumseh Sherman, one of the Union's most respected veteran commanders, has said,

> I have had the question put to me often, 'Is not a negro as good as a white man to stop a bullet?' Yes: and a sand-bag is better; but can a negro do our skirmishing and picket duty? Can they improvise bridges, sorties, flank movements, etc., like the white man? *I* say no.[3]

Such esteemed leaders recognize that blacks, while able to handle simpler tasks, are not adept or experienced enough to tackle the complex demands of frontline combat.

President Lincoln has also been hesitant to authorize the use of black combat troops. He rightly fears that Union soldiers from the border states such as Kansas and Missouri, where sympathy with the South is still prevalent, would react poorly to the notion of black soldiers. In 1862 Mr. Lincoln proclaimed to an Indiana delegation that "to arm the negroes would turn 50,000 bayonets from the loyal Border States against us that were for us."[4] Even in the more recent Emancipation

Proclamation, the president has softened his position, but he has shown that he is still unwilling to send black troops into combat. Instead, the proclamation mandates that black volunteers "of suitable condition will be received into the armed service of the United States to garrison forts, positions, stations, and other places, and to man vessels of all sorts in said service." Even these allowances may alarm conservatives, but clearly the wording of the proclamation indicates that the president is not eager to commit black troops to battle.

Blacks Speak Out Against Enlistment

Abolitionists would argue that these opinions reflect the prejudice of this nation. Yet some of the strongest arguments against organizing black regiments come from the Negroes themselves. Some blacks want nothing to do with a white man's war; others, however, astutely surmise that this war is not about granting the Negro his freedom and citizenship and that taking up arms will not guarantee these rewards. One free black man from Ohio asserted that it was "absurd to suppose that the fact of tendering our services to settle a domestic war when we know that our services will be contemptuously rejected, will not procure a practical acknowledgement of our rights."[5] No duty embraced by the black man, however extreme, can change the character of this war. As the president and his supporters in the North have assured the public, this war has always been about preserving the Union.

Union Above All Else

All of the North's efforts should be directed toward reuniting this great country. The government must weigh its actions with reunion in mind. Many, like Congressman Garrett Davis of Kentucky, believe that sending black troops into the land where many were former slaves can only promise the immediate destruction of the South and ensure future dissension by Southerners, who will not forget those who loosed a tide of vengeful Negroes upon them. As Davis contends,

If you put arms in the hands of the negroes and make them feel their power and impress them with their former slavery, wrongs, and injustice, and arm them . . . , you will whet their fiendish passions, make them the destroying scourge of the cotton States, and you will bring upon the country a condition of things what will render restoration hopeless.[6]

Reconciliation cannot derive from turning slave against master. The aim of this war is to suppress rebellion, not to provide recompense to the Negro for years of enslavement. If the arming of black regiments lacks widespread support in the North, if it threatens to disrupt support from border states, and if it most probably will delay the restoration of the entire Union, then there is no advantage in instituting such a policy. To adopt this plan is to admit that the Negro is the white man's equal and that this war is being fought to promote this ideal. This is an abolitionist agenda, serving the aims of but a few who claim to support the Union cause. Most who sympathize with the Union, however, prefer to believe they are fighting for a grander cause; they are willing to lay down their lives to save the nation, not to save the Negro.

1. Quoted in Hondon B. Hargrove, *Black Union Soldiers in the Civil War.* Jefferson, NC: McFarland, 1988, p. 3.

2. Quoted in James M. McPherson, *Battle Cry of Freedom: The Civil War Era.* New York: Ballantine Books, 1989, p. 502.

3. Quoted in Geoffrey C. Ward with Ric Burns and Ken Burns, *The Civil War: An Illustrated History.* New York: Alfred A. Knopf, 1991, p. 247.

4. Quoted in James M. McPherson, *Ordeal by Fire: The Civil War and Reconstruction.* New York: Alfred A. Knopf, 1982, p. 350.

5. Quoted in Page Smith, *Trial by Fire*, vol. 5 of *A People's History of the Civil War and Reconstruction.* New York: McGraw-Hill, 1982, p. 254.

6. Quoted in William Dudley, ed., *The Civil War: Opposing Viewpoints.* San Diego: Greenhaven Press, 1995, p. 218.

CHAPTER 3

Aftermath

"Treading on the heels of a war that began because of blurred distinctions between the jurisdictions of state and the central governments, President Johnson is determined not to exercise federal authority when it is not sanctioned by the Constitution."

The Government Should Support a Moderate Reconstruction Plan

During the conflict that recently divided the nation, the executive office envisioned only one role for the central government: to restore the Union. As the war raged, President Lincoln held that purpose before all others, and now in peacetime, President Johnson adheres to this guiding principle. Restoring the Union means reconstructing the ruined South and returning it to its rightful place in the Union. The role of government in accomplishing this task is limited. It does not entail the imposition of Northern values on the South or the vengeful destruction of the Southern economy. The government shall simply enforce the Constitution and ensure that the state governments in the South may again participate in the Republic. To venture beyond these obligations is to violate the functions of government and endanger the peaceable mending of this nation.

The Moderate Plan

Following Mr. Lincoln's ideas for rebuilding the South at war's end, President Johnson adopted a plan for Reconstruction that has facilitated reunion. To begin repatriation, he issued the Proclamation of Amnesty, which pardoned most Southerners who fought in the rebellion and returned to them their rights and property. This amnesty, however, came with the condition that the participants take an oath of allegiance and swear to abide by the laws of the nation, especially in regard to the emancipation of slaves. In each Southern state, those loyal citizens chose delegates to attend a convention to amend their state constitutions to align themselves once again with the Republic. With this accomplished the central government was then able to remove its troops and lift martial law from the state. By December 1865 these modest but important achievements had strengthened the Union and the president could declare with pride, "I have . . . gradually and quietly and by almost imperceptible steps, sought to restore the rightful energy of the General Government and of the States."[1]

This moderate Reconstruction strategy has promoted the healing that President Johnson predicted. Testimonials to the plan's success were immediately forthcoming. After a tour of the South, General Ulysses S. Grant determined "that the mass of thinking men of the South accept the present situation of affairs in good faith."[2] And newspaper correspondent Benjamin C. Truman reported that, only a year into Reconstruction, "the great, substantial, and prevailing element [in the South] is more loyal now than it was at the end of the war."[3] Such endorsements bear witness to the smooth transition from animosity to even-temperedness the South has made as a result of President Johnson's program. Everyone is aware of the resentment and hostility that a less competent leader could have aroused with a more radical Reconstruction plan. But knowing when to make strong demands and when to don kid gloves is the sign of an effective president whose policies are concerned with the welfare of the entire nation.

Enfranchising Blacks Is Not a Federal Concern

President Johnson has always been acutely aware of his role in Reconstruction. He understands when to employ federal powers and when to withhold them. Especially treading on the heels of a war that began because of blurred distinctions between the jurisdictions of state and the central governments, President Johnson is determined not to exercise federal authority when it is not sanctioned by the Constitution. For example, the president is not ready to give, by federal decree, freed Negroes the right to vote. President Johnson justly believes that this is not a matter for the central government. He trusts that the states will best determine how to gradually enfranchise the blacks in their jurisdictions. The president rightly fears that extending voting rights by federal order risks two potential crises. First, the enfranchisement of the Negroes may turn a now peaceable South back into a hostile camp. Second, if given the vote, the large populations of blacks in each state would most likely reinstate the Southern-aristocrat governments that led Southern states out of the Union.

Although this latter fear may seem unfounded, one must realize that former slaveholders, who had the power in the states, cared and provided for their slaves. Nonslaveholding whites in the South had no voice in government and now, with emancipation, will be viewed by blacks as nothing more than competition for the agrarian jobs available in the South. As Johnson concludes, "the negro will vote with the late master, whom he does not hate, rather than with the nonslaveholding white, whom he does hate."[4] Thus, the gentrified governments that ran Southern states into troubled waters will, with the aid of the black vote, be at their helms again.

Maintaining the Separation of State and Federal Authority

Furthermore, to try and guarantee the civil rights of the black voter would place too much power in the hands of the central government. Since black civil rights are not ensured by the Constitution, President Johnson warns that this move can only be interpreted as another "stride toward centralization, and the concentration of all legislative powers in the national

Government."[5] Such centralization brought about the divisive arguments that led to secession. President Johnson recognizes that states must be allowed the power to legislate matters not directly covered by the Constitution. It is the elected state officials who will best determine the most beneficial ways to contend with their citizens.

President Johnson's moderate plan for Reconstruction has already accomplished its political goals. The people of the South have sworn allegiance to the Constitution, new state governments have been formed, and slavery has been abolished. And all of this has been achieved without inspiring further animosity during this tense period of rebuilding and reconciliation. The peaceable acceptance of these measures has primarily been due to the president's refusal to overstep his authority as proscribed by the Constitution. As any citizen would expect, President Johnson believes his duty is to make sure that all people, including himself, are bound by the Constitution. "The Union and the Constitution are inseparable. As long as one is obeyed by all parties, the other will be preserved; and if one is destroyed, both must perish together."[6]

1.   Quoted in Avery Craven, *Reconstruction: The Ending of the Civil War.* New York: Holt, Rinehart, and Winston, 1969, p. 92.

2.   Quoted in Kenneth M. Stampp, *The Era of Reconstruction, 1865–1877.* New York: Alfred A. Knopf, 1965, p. 73.

3.   Quoted in Stampp, *The Era of Reconstruction,* p. 73.

4.   Quoted in Eric Foner, *A Short History of Reconstruction, 1863–1877.* New York: Harper & Row, 1990, p. 85.

5.   Quoted in Foner, *A Short History of Reconstruction,* p. 113.

6.   Quoted in William Dudley, ed., *The Civil War: Opposing Viewpoints.* San Diego: Greenhaven Press, 1995, p. 44.

"This administration cannot act halfheartedly in carrying out its plans to reconstruct the South, nor can it overlook the trespasses of the rebel states as radical changes are instituted."

The Government Should Opt for a Radical Reconstruction Plan

The Union has just won a glorious victory over a rebellious South. The ideals that fostered dissent and ultimately secession have been defeated. During this period of Reconstruction, it is imperative that those factors that caused the great division do not again interfere with the longevity of the nation. To ensure this, the North must be strict in dealing with the South; it would be an insult to those who fought and died for the Union if the South were forgiven without being compelled to make amends for its treasonous acts.

Moderate Reconstruction Is Too Lenient

President Johnson has already instituted his Reconstruction program, but his lenient policies are not aimed at purging the South of the beliefs that brought about war. He has tried to be amicable, allowing Southern representatives to resume their seats in Congress, pardoning the rebel aristocracy and letting them reign again in their individual states, and either remaining noncommittal or standing openly antagonistic to the notion of black enfranchisement. In effect, he is reinstating the antebellum South when he should be acting decisively to create a new republic based on the principles for which Union men gave their lives. As in any war, the victors earn the right to rule, or in the words of an 1865 editorial in the New York *Independent*, "The North must remain the absolute Dictator of the Republic until the spirit of the North shall become the spirit of the whole country."[1] If the president continues to be lenient, he will invite another war over the very same controversies that so recently inspired rebellion.

The South Should Be Purged of Its Treasonous Ways

It is time for the government to take a strong hand in reshaping the South. This means a quick dismantling of the plantation system that elevated the Southern gentry at the expense of the black slave. As Congressman Thaddeus Stevens declares,

Thaddeus Stevens

The whole fabric of southern society *must* be changed, and never can it be done if this opportunity is lost. . . . How can republican institutions, free schools, free churches, free social intercourse exist in a mingled community of nabobs [aristocrats] and serfs [slaves]?[2]

Perhaps, as Congressman Stevens advocates, the Union should confiscate Southern land and then parcel it up among the former slaves. Many legislators are behind this type of retribution. Indeed, the government has the right to demand such drastic change; without leveling demands, Union men may rightly ask what was achieved by victory? If the South is reinstated without penalty, without contrition, then Southerners have learned nothing from their treason.

Negroes Should Be Given the Rights of White Citizens

To strike down the Old South and bury its divisive heritage, the government must ensure that the black populations made free by the war will be free in deed and not just in word. To raise the former slave out of his subservient position, he must be made equal to the white Southerner. Senator Henry Wilson makes clear the course this nation must take:

> We must see to it that the man made free by the Constitution . . . is a freeman indeed; that he can go where he pleases, work when and for whom he pleases; . . . that he can lease and buy and sell and own property, real and personal; that he can go into the schools and educate himself and his children; that the rights and guarantees of the . . . common law are his, and that he walks the earth, proud and erect in the conscious dignity of a free man.[3]

Guaranteeing the Negro his civil rights will help break the grip of the white Southerner who profits by keeping the Negro in servitude and ignorance. A civil rights bill has been laid before the president, but he has vetoed it to the dismay of most congressmen. Although the president's veto was disheartening, ensuring civil rights would not have been adequate to equate the races in the South. Giving a freeman education and property is inconsequential if he is not also given the vote. Only by enfranchising the Negroes can the true character of Southern society be amended.

Without Negro Enfranchisement the Old South Will Remain

Given his rejection of the civil rights bill, it is not surprising that President Johnson has not been willing to support the enfranchisement of blacks. Of course, by pardoning the white power structure in the South and keeping it alive, he can count on its support in the next presidential election. Giving the Negro the vote will upset the balance of power in the South; it will allow the black man to change things according to his best interests. As Frederick Douglass avows,

> The true way and the easiest way is to make our government entirely consistent with itself, and give to every loyal citizen the elective franchise,—a right and power which will be ever present, and will form a wall of fire for his protection.[4]

If this nation does not adopt a Reconstruction plan that will deliver the ballot to the former slave, then the former masters will return to their political posts. Congressman Stevens foretells, "If [Negro] suffrage is excluded in the rebel States then every one of them is sure to send a solid rebel representative delegation to Congress."[5] Flooding Congress with former secessionists and slaveholders is sure to cause the obstruction or strangulation of any legislation hinting at overturning the Old South. What hope of black enfranchisement would exist then? What guarantee would there be that the secessionist mindset would ever be changed?

The Government Is Justified in Enacting Change in the South

This administration cannot act halfheartedly in carrying out its plans to reconstruct the South, nor can it overlook the trespasses of the rebel states as radical changes are instituted. The president seems too willing to curry favor with the Southern elite, and too unwilling to destroy the system that will forever try to keep one class of people in bondage. Perhaps he has forgotten that the Union was set upon by the South, and he is now justified in taking measures both to protect against further rebellion and to ensure that civil rights are extended to all people of this nation. After evaluating the reasonableness of requiring drastic changes in the part of the nation that instigated civil war, the Joint Committee of Congress on Reconstruction declared,

"A government thus outraged had a perfect right to exact indemnity for the injuries done, and security against the recurrence of such outrages in the future."[6] It is time for the government to use this right and make the changes that will guarantee the security of the entire nation.

1. Quoted in Avery Craven, *Reconstruction: The Ending of the Civil War.* New York: Holt, Rinehart, and Winston, 1969, p. 93.

2. Quoted in Eric Foner, *A Short History of Reconstruction, 1863–1877.* New York: Harper & Row, 1990, p. 107.

3. Quoted in Kenneth M. Stampp, *The Era of Reconstruction, 1865–1877.* New York: Alfred A. Knopf, 1965, p. 88.

4. Quoted in Harvey Wish, ed., *Reconstruction in the South, 1865–1877.* New York: Noonday Press, 1966, p. 83.

5. Quoted in Stampp, *The Era of Reconstruction,* p. 93.

6. Quoted in Craven, *Reconstruction,* p. 161.

APPENDIX

Original Documents Pertaining to the Civil War

Document 1: Lincoln's House Divided Speech

In 1858 the Republican state convention nominated Abraham Lincoln to run against Stephen A. Douglas for the U.S. Senate. On June 16 Lincoln accepted the honor with a speech that caused considerable controversy, a portion of which is presented here. While some praised the speech as a clear summation of the issues facing the nation, many accused Lincoln of exacerbating the conflict between the North and the South.

Mr. President and Gentlemen of the Convention.

If we could first know *where* we are, and *whither* we are tending, we could then better judge *what* to do, and *how* to do it.

We are now far into the *fifth* year, since a policy was initiated, with the *avowed* object, and *confident* promise, of putting an end to slavery agitation.

Under the operation of that policy, that agitation has not only, *not ceased*, but has *constantly augmented*.

In *my* opinion, it *will* not cease, until a *crisis* shall have been reached, and passed.

"A house divided against itself cannot stand."

I believe this government cannot endure, permanently half *slave* and half *free*.

I do not expect the Union to be *dissolved*—I do not expect the house to *fall*—but I *do* expect it will cease to be divided.

It will become *all* one thing, or *all* the other.

Either the *opponents* of slavery, will arrest the further spread of it, and place it where the public mind shall rest in the belief that it is in the course of ultimate extinction; or its *advocates* will push it forward, till it shall become alike lawful in *all* the States, *old* as well as *new*—*North* as well as *South*.

Abraham Lincoln, "The House Divided Speech," in Mario M. Cuomo and Harold Holzer, eds., *Lincoln on Democracy*. New York: A Cornelia & Michael Bessie Book, 1990, pp. 105–106.

Document 2: The Gettysburg Address

On November 19, 1863, four months after the Union repulsed the Confederacy at the Battle of Gettysburg, President Lincoln addressed a crowd of thousands that had gathered in the small town in Pennsylvania for the dedication of a cemetery to the soldiers who had lost their lives there. Legend has it that Lincoln composed the now-famous speech on his train ride the day before and that it was poorly received by his audience, but historians point to evidence refuting both claims.

Four score and seven years ago our fathers brought forth on this continent, a new nation, conceived in Liberty, and dedicated to the proposition that all men are created equal.

Now we are engaged in a great civil war, testing whether that nation, or any nation so conceived and so dedicated, can long endure. We are met on a great battle-field of that war. We have come to dedicate a portion of that field, as a final resting place for those who here gave their lives that that nation might live. It is altogether fitting and proper that we should do this.

But, in a larger sense, we can not dedicate—we can not consecrate—we can not hallow—this ground. The brave men, living and dead, who struggled here have consecrated it, far above our poor power to add or detract. The world will little note, nor long remember what we say here, but it can never forget what they did here. It is for us the living, rather, to be dedicated here to the unfinished work which they who fought here have thus far so nobly advanced. It is rather for us to be here dedicated to the great task remaining before us—that from these honored dead we take increased devotion to that cause for which they gave the last full measure of devotion—that we here highly resolve that these dead shall not have died in vain—that this nation, under God, shall have a new birth of freedom—and that government of the people, by the people, for the people, shall not perish from the earth.

Abraham Lincoln, "The Gettysburg Address," in Mario M. Cuomo and Harold Holzer, eds., *Lincoln on Democracy*. New York: A Cornelia & Michael Bessie Book, 1990, pp. 307–308.

Document 3: Robert E. Lee Bids His Troops Farewell

On April 10, 1865, the day after he surrendered to Ulysses S. Grant at the Appomattox Court House in Virginia, Confederate general Robert E. Lee issued his last orders to his troops.

After four years of arduous service, marked by unsurpassed courage and fortitude, the Army of Northern Virginia has been compelled to yield to overwhelming numbers and resources.

I need not tell the brave survivors of so many hard fought battles, who have remained steadfast to the last, that I have consented to the results from no distrust of them.

But feeling that valor and devotion could accomplish nothing that would compensate for the loss that must have attended the continuance of the contest, I determined to avoid the useless sacrifice of those whose past services have endeared them to their countrymen.

By the terms of the agreement officers and men can return to their homes. . . . You will take with you the satisfaction that proceeds from the consciousness of duty faithfully performed, and I earnestly pray that a Merciful God will extend to you His blessing and protection.

With an increasing admiration of your constancy and devotion to your country, and a grateful remembrance of your kind and generous considerations for myself, I bid you all an affectionate farewell.

Robert E. Lee, "A Fond Farewell," in William Dudley, ed., *The Civil War*. San Diego: Greenhaven Press, 1995, p. 258.

Document 4: South Carolina Secedes

On December 20, 1860, in response to Abraham Lincoln's election as president, South Carolina became the first state to secede from the United States. The state's legislature presented its reasons for seceding in the form of a declaration (issued in 1862), some of which is presented here. It argues that the United States is a union of sovereign states and that states have the right to withdraw from that union if any of its member states do not fulfill their obligations to the Constitution. The declaration lists its grievances against the Northern states, which it believes have violated the Constitution.

The people of the state of South Carolina, in convention assembled, on the 26th day of April, A.D. 1852, declared that the frequent violations of the Constitution of the United States by the federal government, and its encroachments upon the reserved rights of the states, fully justified this state in their withdrawal from the federal Union; but in deference to the opinions and wishes of the other slaveholding states, she forbore at that time to exercise this right. Since that time, these encroachments have continued to increase, and further forbearance ceases to be a virtue.

And, now, the state of South Carolina, having resumed her separate and equal place among nations, deems it due to herself, to the remaining United States of America, and to the nations of the world, that she should declare the immediate causes which have led to this act.

In the year 1765, that portion of the British empire embracing Great Britain undertook to make laws for the government of that portion composed of the thirteen American colonies. A struggle for the right of self-government ensued, which resulted, on the 4th of July, 1776, in a Declaration, by the colonies, "that they are, and of right ought to be, *free and independent states*; and that, as free and independent states, they have full power to levy war, conclude peace, contract alliances, establish commerce, and to do all other acts and things which independent states may of right do."

They further solemnly declared that whenever any "form of government becomes destructive of the ends for which it was established, it is the right of the people to alter or abolish it, and to institute a new government." Deeming the government of Great Britain to have become destructive of these ends, they declared that the colonies "are absolved from all allegiance to the British Crown, and that all political connection between them and the state of Great Britain is, and ought to be, totally dissolved."

In pursuance of this Declaration of Independence, each of the thirteen states proceeded to exercise its separate sovereignty; adopted for itself a constitution, and appointed officers for the administration of government in all its departments—Legislative, Executive, and Judicial. For purposes of defense, they united their arms and their counsels, and, in 1778, they entered into a league known as the Articles of Confederation, whereby they agreed to entrust the administration of their external relations to a common agent, known as the Congress of the United States, expressly declaring, in the 1st Article, "that each state retains its sovereignty, freedom, and independence, and every power, jurisdiction, and right which is not, by this Confederation, expressly delegated to the United States in Congress assembled.". . .

In 1787, deputies were appointed by the states to revise the Articles of Confederation; and on Sept. 17, 1787, these deputies recommended, for the adoption of the states, the Articles of Union, known as the Constitution of the United States.

The parties to whom this Constitution was submitted were the several sovereign states; they were to agree or disagree, and when nine of them agreed, the compact was to take effect among those concurring; and the general government, as the common agent, was then to be invested with their authority.

If only nine of the thirteen states had concurred, the other four would have remained as they then were—separate, sovereign states, independent of any of the provisions of the Constitution. In fact, two of the states did not accede to the Constitution until long after it had gone into operation among the other eleven; and during that interval, they each exercised the functions of an independent nation.

By this Constitution, certain duties were imposed upon the several states, and the exercise of certain of their powers was restrained, which necessarily impelled their continued existence as sovereign states. But, to remove all doubt, an amendment was added which declared that the powers not delegated to the United States by the Constitution, nor prohibited by it to the states, are reserved to the states respectively, or to the people. On the 23rd of May, 1788, South Carolina, by a convention of her people, passed an ordinance assenting to this Constitution, and afterward altered her own constitution to conform herself to the obligations she had undertaken.

Thus was established, by compact between the states, a government with defined objects and powers, limited to the express words of the grant. This limitation left the whole remaining mass of power subject to the clause reserving it to the states or the people, and rendered unnecessary any specification of reserved rights. We hold that the government thus established is subject to the two great principles asserted in the Declaration of Independence; and we hold further that the mode of its formation subjects it to a third fundamental principle, namely, the law of compact. We maintain that in every compact between two or more parties, the obligation is mutual; that the failure of one of the contracting parties to perform a material part of the agreement entirely releases the obligation of the other; and that, where no arbiter is provided, each party is remitted to his own judgment to determine the fact of failure, with all its consequences.

In the present case, the fact is established with certainty. We assert that fourteen of the states have deliberately refused for years past to fulfill their constitutional obligations, and we refer to their own statutes for the proof.

The Constitution of the United States, in its 4th Article, provides as follows: "No person held to service or labor in one state, under the laws thereof, escaping into another shall, in consequence of any law or regulation therein, be discharged from such service or labor, but shall be delivered up, on claim of the party to whom such service or labor may be due."

This stipulation was so material to the compact that without it that compact would not have been made. The greater number of the contracting parties held slaves, and they had previously evinced their estimate of the value of such a stipulation by making it a condition in the ordinance for the government of the territory ceded by Virginia, which obligations, and the laws of the general government, have ceased to effect the objects of the Constitution. The states of Maine, New Hampshire, Vermont, Massachusetts, Connecticut, Rhode Island, New York, Pennsylvania, Illinois, Indiana, Michigan, Wisconsin, and Iowa have enacted laws which either nullify the acts of Congress or render useless any attempt to execute them. In many of these states the fugitive is discharged from the service of labor claimed, and in none of them has the state government complied with the stipulation made in the Constitution. . . .

Thus the constitutional compact has been deliberately broken and disregarded by the nonslaveholding states; and the consequence follows that South Carolina is released from her obligation.

The ends for which this Constitution was framed are declared by itself to be "to form a more perfect union, to establish justice, insure domestic tranquillity, provide for the common defense, promote the general welfare, and secure the blessings of liberty to ourselves and our posterity." These ends it endeavored to accomplish by a federal government in which each state was recognized as an equal and had separate control over its own institutions. The right of property in slaves was recognized by giving to free persons distinct political rights; by giving them the right to represent, and burdening them with direct taxes for, three-fifths of their slaves; by authorizing the importation of slaves for twenty years; and by stipulating for the rendition of fugitives from labor.

We affirm that these ends for which this government was instituted have been defeated, and the government itself has been destructive of them by the action of the nonslaveholding states. Those states have assumed the right of deciding upon the propriety of our domestic institutions; and have denied the rights of property established in fifteen of the states and recognized by the Constitution. They have denounced as sinful the institution of slavery; they have permitted the open establishment among them of societies, whose avowed object is to disturb the peace of and eloign the property of the citizens of other states. They have encouraged and assisted thousands of our slaves to leave their homes; and, those who remain, have been incited by emissaries, books, and pictures to servile insurrection.

For twenty-five years this agitation has been steadily increasing, until it has now secured to its aid the power of the common government. Observing the *forms* of the Constitution, a sectional party has found, within that article establishing the Executive Department, the means of subverting the Constitution itself. A geographical line has been drawn across the Union, and all the states north of that line have united in the election of a man to the high office of President of the United States whose opinions and purposes are hostile to slavery. He is to be entrusted with the administration of the common government, because he has declared that "Government cannot endure permanently half slave, half free," and that the public mind must rest in the belief that slavery is in the course of ultimate extinction. . . .

On the 4th of March next this party will take possession of the government. It has announced that the South shall be excluded from the common territory, that the judicial tribunal shall be made sectional, and that a war must be waged against slavery until it shall cease throughout the United States.

The guarantees of the Constitution will then no longer exist; the equal rights of the states will be lost. The slaveholding states will no longer have the power of self-government or self-protection, and the federal government will have become their enemy.

Sectional interest and animosity will deepen the irritation; and all hope of remedy is rendered vain by the fact that the public opinion at the North has invested a great political error with the sanctions of a more erroneous religious belief.

We, therefore, the people of South Carolina, by our delegates in convention assembled, appealing to the Supreme Judge of the world for the rectitude of our intentions, have solemnly declared that the Union heretofore existing between this state and the other states of North America is dissolved; and that the state of South Carolina has resumed her position among the nations of the world, as [a] separate and independent state, with full power to levy war, conclude peace, contract alliances, establish commerce, and to do all other acts and things which independent states may of right do.

South Carolina Declaration, "Secession Is Justified," in William Dudley, ed., *The Civil War.* San Diego: Greenhaven Press, 1995, pp. 117–22.

Document 5: States Do Not Have a Right to Secede

The Southern states that seceded and formed the Confederate States of America did so in the four months between Abraham Lincoln's election as president and his inauguration on March 4, 1861. (Lincoln's predecessor, James Buchanan, had not acted to prevent the states from seceding.) In the parts of his inaugural speech reprinted below, Lincoln addresses the seceded states. He seeks to placate them but maintains that they have no legal right to secede. Northerners generally viewed the speech as conciliatory, while many Southerners felt it was a declaration of war on the Confederacy.

Fellow Citizens of the United States:

In compliance with a custom as old as the government itself, I appear before you to address you briefly and to take, in your presence, the oath prescribed by the Constitution of the United States to be taken by the President "before he enters on the execution of his office."

I do not consider it necessary, at present, for me to discuss those matters of administration about which there is no special anxiety or excitement. Apprehension seems to exist among the people of the Southern states that, by the accession of a Republican administration, their property and their peace and personal security are to be endangered. There has never been any reasonable cause for such apprehension. Indeed, the most ample evidence to the contrary has all the while existed and been open to their inspection. It is found in nearly all the published speeches of him who now addresses you.

I do but quote from one of those speeches when I declare that "I have no purpose, directly or indirectly, to interfere with the institution of slavery in the states where it exists. I believe I have no lawful right to do so, and I have no inclination to do so." Those who nominated and elected me did so with full knowledge that I had made this and many similar declarations, and had never recanted them. And, more than this, they placed in the platform, for my acceptance, and as a law to themselves and to me, the clear and emphatic resolution which I now read:

Resolved, that the maintenance inviolate of the rights of the states, and especially the right of each state, to order and control its own domestic institutions according to its own judgment exclusively is essential to that balance of power on which the perfection and endurance of our political fabric depend; and we denounce the lawless invasion by armed force of the soil of any state or territory, no matter under what pretext, as among the gravest of crimes.

I now reiterate these sentiments; and in doing so, I only press upon the public attention the most conclusive evidence, of which the case is susceptible, that the property, peace, and security of no section are to be in any way endangered by the now incoming administration. I add, too, that all the protection which, consistently with the Constitution and the laws, can be given will be cheerfully given to all the states when lawfully demanded, for whatever cause—as cheerfully to one section as to another.

There is much controversy about the delivering up of fugitives from service or labor. The clause I now read is as plainly written in the Constitution as any other of its provisions:

No person held to service or labor in one state, under the laws thereof, escaping into another, shall, in consequence of any law or regulation therein, be discharged from such service or labor, but shall be delivered up on claim of the party to whom such service or labor may be due.

It is scarcely questioned that this provision was intended by those who made it for the reclaiming of what we call fugitive slaves; and the intention of the lawgiver is the law. . . .

I take the official oath today with no mental reservations and with no purpose to construe the Constitution or laws by any hypercritical rules. And while I do not choose now to specify particular acts of Congress as proper to be enforced, I do suggest that it will be much safer for all, both in official and private stations, to conform to and abide by all those acts which stand unrepealed than to violate any of them, trusting to find impunity in having them held to be unconstitutional. . . .

I hold that, in contemplation of universal law and of the Constitution, the Union of these states is perpetual. Perpetuity is implied, if not expressed, in the fundamental law of all national governments. It is safe to assert that no government proper ever had a provision in its organic law for its own termination. Continue to execute all the express provisions of our national Constitution, and the Union will endure forever—it being impossible to destroy it except by some action not provided for in the instrument itself.

Again, if the United States be not a government proper, but an association of states in the nature of contract merely, can it, as a contract, be peaceably unmade by less than all the parties who made it? One party to a contract may violate it—break it, so to speak—but does it not require all to lawfully rescind it? Descending from these general principles, we find the proposition that in legal contemplation, the Union is perpetual, confirmed by the history of the Union itself.

The Union is much older than the Constitution. It was formed, in fact, by the Articles of Association in 1774. It was matured and continued by the Declaration of Independence in 1776. It was further matured, and the faith of all the then thirteen states expressedly plighted and engaged, that it should be perpetual by the Articles of Confederation of 1778. And finally, in 1787, one of the declared objects for ordaining and establishing the Constitution, was "*to form a more perfect Union.*"

But if destruction of the Union by one or by a part only of the states be lawfully possible, the Union is *less* perfect than before the Constitution, having lost the vital element of perpetuity.

It follows from these views that no state, upon its own mere motion, can lawfully get out of the Union—that *resolves* and *ordinances* to that effect are legally void; and that acts of violence within any state or states against the authority of the United States are insurrectionary or revolutionary, according to circumstances.

I therefore consider that, in view of the Constitution and the laws, the Union is unbroken; and to the extent of my ability, I shall take care, as the Constitution itself expressly enjoins upon me, that the laws of the Union be faithfully executed in all the states. Doing this I deem to be only a simple duty on my part; and I shall perform it, so far as practicable, unless my rightful masters, the American people, shall withhold the requisite means or in some authoritative manner direct the contrary. . . .

All profess to be content in the Union if all constitutional rights can be maintained. Is it true, then, that any right plainly written in the Constitution has been denied? I think not. Happily, the human mind is so constituted that no party can reach to the audacity of doing this. Think, if you can, of a single instance in which a plainly written provision of the Constitution has ever been denied. If, by the mere force of numbers, a majority should deprive a minority of any clearly written constitutional right, it might, in a moral point of view, justify revolution—certainly would, if such right were a vital one. But such is not our case.

All the vital rights of minorities and of individuals are so plainly assured to them by affirmations and negations, guarantees and prohibitions, in the Constitution that controversies never arise concerning them. But no organic law can ever be framed with a provision specifically applicable to every question which may occur in practical administration. No foresight can anticipate nor any document of reasonable length contain express provisions for all possible questions. Shall fugitives from labor be surrendered by national or by state authority? The Constitution does not expressly say. *May* Congress prohibit slavery in the territories? The Constitution does not expressly say. *Must* Congress protect slavery in the territories? The Constitution does not expressly say.

From questions of this class spring all our constitutional controversies, and we divide upon them into majorities and minorities. If the minority will not acquiesce, the majority must, or the government must cease. There is no other alternative; for continuing the government is acquiescence on one side or the other. If a minority, in such case, will secede rather than acquiesce, they make a precedent which in turn will divide and ruin them; for a minority of their own will secede from them whenever a majority refuses to be controlled by such minority.

For instance, why may not any portion of a new confederacy, a year or two hence, arbitrarily secede again, precisely as portions of the present Union now claim to secede from it? All who cherish disunion sentiments are now being educated to the exact temper of doing this. Is there such perfect identity of interests among the states to compose a new Union as to produce harmony only and prevent renewed secession?

Plainly, the central idea of secession is the essence of anarchy. A majority, held in restraint by constitutional checks and limitations, and always changing easily with deliberate changes of popular opinions and sentiments, is the only true sovereign of a free people. Whoever rejects it does of necessity fly to anarchy or to despotism. Unanimity is impossible. The rule of a minority, as a permanent arrangement, is wholly inadmissible; so that, rejecting the majority principle, anarchy or despotism in some form is all that is left. . . .

Physically speaking, we cannot separate. We cannot remove our respective sections from each other, nor build an impassable wall between them. A husband and wife may be divorced, and go out of the presence and beyond the reach of each other, but the different parts of our country cannot do this. They cannot but remain face to face; and intercourse, either amicable or hostile, must continue between them. Is it possible, then, to make that intercourse more advantageous or more satisfactory *after* separation than *before?* Can aliens make treaties easier than friends can make laws? Can treaties be more faithfully enforced between aliens than laws can among friends? Suppose you go to war, you cannot fight always; and when, after much loss on both sides and no gain on either, you cease fighting, the identical old questions as to terms of intercourse are again upon you.

This country, with its institutions, belongs to the people who inhabit it. Whenever they shall grow weary of the existing government, they can exercise their *constitutional* right of amending it or their *revolutionary* right to dismember or overthrow it. I cannot be ignorant of the fact that many worthy and patriotic citizens are desirous of having the national Constitution amended. While I make no recommendation of amendments, I fully recognize the rightful authority of the people over the whole subject, to be exercised in either of the modes prescribed in the instrument itself; and I should, under existing circumstances, favor rather than oppose a fair opportunity being afforded the people to act upon it. . . .

The chief magistrate derives all his authority from the people, and they have conferred none upon him to fix terms for their separation of the states. The people themselves can do this also if they choose; but the executive, as such, has nothing to do with it. His duty is to administer the present government, as it came to his hands, and to transmit it, unimpaired by him, to his successor. Why should there not be a patient confidence in the ultimate justice of the people? Is there any better or equal hope in the world? In our present differences, is either party without faith of being in the right? . . .

Such of you as are now dissatisfied still have the old Constitution unimpaired, and, on the sensitive point, the laws of your own framing under it; while the new administration will have no immediate power, if it would, to change either.

If it were admitted that you who are dissatisfied hold the right side in the dispute, there still is no single good reason for precipitate action. Intelligence, patriotism, Christianity, and a firm reliance on Him, who has never yet forsaken this favored land, are still competent to adjust, in the best way, all our present difficulty.

In *your* hands, my dissatisfied fellow countrymen, and not in *mine* is the momentous issue of civil war. The government will not assail *you.* You can have no conflict without being yourselves the aggressors. *You* have no oath registered in heaven to destroy the government, while *I* shall have the most solemn one to "preserve, protect, and defend" it.

I am loathe to close. We are not enemies but friends. We must not be enemies. Though passion may have strained, it must not break our bonds of affection.

The mystic chords of memory, stretching from every battlefield and patriot grave to every living heart and hearthstone all over this broad land, will yet swell the chorus of the Union, when again touched, as surely they will be, by the better angels of our nature.

Abraham Lincoln, "First Inaugural Address," in William Dudley, ed., *The Civil War*. San Diego: Greenhaven Press, 1995, pp. 124–33.

Document 6: George McDuffie Defends Slavery

In 1835, as slavery was becoming an increasingly divisive issue, South Carolina governor George McDuffie defended the practice in a speech to the state legislature. In this part of the speech, McDuffie claims that slavery is a positive good rather than a necessary evil, and many of the ideas he expresses were popular among slavery's advocates.

No human institution, in my opinion, is more manifestly consistent with the will of God than domestic slavery, and no one of His ordinances is written in more legible characters than that which consigns the African race to this condition, as more conducive to their own happiness, than any other of which they are susceptible. Whether we consult the sacred Scriptures or the lights of nature and reason, we shall find these truths as abundantly apparent as if written with a sunbeam in the heavens. Under both the Jewish and Christian dispensations of our religion, domestic slavery existed with the unequivocal sanction of its prophets, its apostles, and finally its great Author. The patriarchs themselves, those chosen instruments of God, were slaveholders. In fact, the divine sanction of this institution is so plainly written that "he who runs may read" it, and those overrighteous pretenders and Pharisees who affect to be scandalized by its existence among us would do well to inquire how much more nearly they walk in the ways of godliness than did Abraham, Isaac, and Jacob.

That the African Negro is destined by Providence to occupy this condition of servile dependence is not less manifest. It is marked on the face, stamped on the skin, and evinced by the intellectual inferiority and natural improvidence of this race. They have all the qualities that fit them for slaves, and not one of those that would fit them to be freemen. They are utterly unqualified, not only for rational freedom but for self-government of any kind. They are, in all respects, physical, moral, and political, inferior to millions of the human race who have for consecutive ages dragged out a wretched existence under a grinding political despotism, and who are doomed to this hopeless condition by the very qualities which unfit them for a better. It is utterly astonishing that any enlightened American, after contemplating all the manifold forms in which even the white race of mankind is doomed to slavery and oppression, should suppose it possible to reclaim the African race from their destiny.

George McDuffie, "Slavery Is Just," in William Dudley, ed., *Slavery*. San Diego: Greenhaven Press, 1992, pp. 66–67.

Document 7: William Lloyd Garrison Condemns Slavery

William Lloyd Garrison was a journalist who became famous for his controversial denunciations of slavery; he was one of the first abolitionists to demand an immediate, rather than a gradual, end to the institution. Garrison's passionate feelings about slavery are evident in this excerpt from an 1860 publication of the American Anti-Slavery Society, the abolitionist organization he founded in 1832.

The one great, distinctive, all-conquering sin in America is its system of chattel slavery—co-existent with the settlement of the country—for a considerable time universally diffused—at first, tolerated as a necessary evil—subsequently, deplored as a calamity—now, defended in every slave state as a most beneficent institution, upheld by natural and revealed religion—in its feebleness, able to dictate terms in the formation of the Constitution—in its strength, controlling parties and sects, courts and legislative assemblies, the army and navy, Congress, the National Executive, the Supreme Court—and having at its disposal all the offices, honors and revenues of the government, wherewith to defy all opposition, and to extend its dominion indefinitely. Gradually abolished in six of the thirteen states which formed the Union, it has concentrated itself in the southern and southwestern portion of the Republic, covering more than one-half of the national territory, and aiming at universal empire.

The victims of this terrible system being of African extraction, it has engendered and established a complexional caste, unknown to European civilization; pervading all parts of the United States like a malaria-tainted atmosphere; in its development, more malignant at the North than at the South; poisoning the life-blood of the most refined and the most depraved alike; and making the remotest connection with the colored race a leprous taint. Its spirit is as brutal as it is unnatural; as mean as it is wicked; as relentless as it is monstrous. It is capable of committing any outrage upon the person, mind or estate of the negro, whether bond or free. . . . No religious creed, no form of worship, no evangelical discipline, no heretical liberality, either mitigates or restrains it. Christian and Infidel, Calvinist and Universalist, Trinitarian and Unitarian, Episcopalian and Methodist, Baptist and Swendenborgian, Old School and New School Presbyterian, Orthodox and Hicksite Quaker, all are infected by it, and equally ready to make an innocent natural distinction the badge of eternal infamy, and a warrant for the most cruel proscription. As a nation sows, so shall it also reap. The retributive justice of God was never more strikingly manifested than in this all-pervading negrophobia, the dreadful consequence of chattel slavery.

William Lloyd Garrison, "The Burden of All Reformers," in David Brion Davis, *Antebellum American Culture: An Interpretive Anthology*. University Park, PA: Pennsylvania State University Press, 1979, pp. 420–21.

Document 8: The Emancipation Proclamation

On September 22, 1862, five days after the Battle of Antietam, President Abraham Lincoln issued a preliminary proclamation stating that he would free all slaves in the rebelling states if the states did not return to the Union by January 1, 1863. They did not, and on that date he issued the following proclamation. It declared freedom for slaves in all areas of the Confederacy that were still in rebellion against the Union. The proclamation also provided for the use of blacks in the Union army and navy. Although the proclamation excluded slaves in border states and Union-controlled areas such as Tennessee and parts of Louisiana and Virginia, it led to the Thirteenth Amendment, which ended slavery in all parts of the United States and was passed on December 18, 1865.

Whereas, on the twenty-second day of September, in the year of our Lord one thousand eight hundred and sixty-two, a proclamation was issued by the President of the United States, containing, among other things, the following, to wit:

That on the 1st day of January, in the year of our Lord one thousand eight hundred and sixty-three, all persons held as slaves within any State, or designated part of a State, the people whereof shall then be in rebellion against the United States, shall be then, thenceforward, and forever free; and the Executive Government of the United States, including the military and naval authority thereof, will recognize and maintain the freedom of such persons, and will do no act or acts to repress such persons, or any of them, in any efforts they may make for their actual freedom.

That the Executive will, on the first day of January aforesaid, by proclamation, designate the States and parts of States, if any, in which the people thereof respectively shall then be in rebellion against the United States; and the fact that any State, or the people thereof, shall on that day be in good faith represented in the Congress of the United States by members chosen thereto at elections wherein a majority of the qualified voters of such States shall have participated, shall in the absence of strong countervailing testimony be deemed conclusive evidence that such State and the people thereof are not then in rebellion against the United States.

Now, therefore, I, Abraham Lincoln, President of the United States, by virtue of the power in me vested as Commander-in-Chief of the Army and Navy of the United States, in time of actual armed rebellion against the authority and government of the United States, and as a fit and necessary war measure for suppressing said rebellion, do on this first day of January, in the year of our Lord one thousand eight hundred and sixty-three, and

in accordance with my purpose so to do, publicly proclaimed for the full period of 100 days from the day first above mentioned, order and designate as
the States and parts of States wherein the people thereof, respectively, are
this day in rebellion against the United States, the following, to wit:
  Arkansas, Texas, Louisiana (except the parishes of St. Bernard, Plaque-
mines, Jefferson, St. John, St. Charles, St. James, Ascension, Assumption,
Terrebonne, Lafourche, St. Mary, St. Martin, and Orleans, including the
city of New Orleans), Mississippi, Alabama, Florida, Georgia, South Carolina, North Carolina, and Virginia (except the forty-eight counties designated as West Virginia, and also the counties of Berkeley, Accomac,
Northampton, Elizabeth City, York, Princess Anne, and Norfolk, including the cities of Norfolk and Portsmouth), and which excepted parts are
for the present left precisely as if this proclamation were not issued.
  And by virtue of the power and for the purpose aforesaid, I do order and
declare that all persons held as slaves within said designated States and
parts of States are, and henceforward shall be, free; and that the Executive
Government of the United States, including the military and naval authorities thereof, shall recognize and maintain the freedom of said persons.
  And I hereby enjoin upon the people so declared to be free to abstain from
all violence, unless in necessary self-defense; and I recommend to them that,
in all cases where allowed, they labor faithfully for reasonable wages.
  And I further declare and make known that such persons of suitable
condition will be received into the armed service of the United States to
garrison forts, positions, stations, and other places, and to man vessels of
all sorts in said service.
  And upon this act, sincerely believed to be an act of justice, warranted
by the Constitution upon military necessity, I invoke the considerate judgment of mankind and the gracious favor of Almighty God.
  In witness whereof, I have hereunto set my hand and caused the seal of
the United States to be affixed.
  Done at the city of Washington, the first day of January, in the year of
our Lord one thousand eight hundred and sixty-three, and of the independence of the United States of America the eighty-seventh.
  By the President: Abraham Lincoln
      William H. Seward, Secretary of State

Abraham Lincoln, "The Emancipation Proclamation," in *The World Book Encyclopedia*, 1993, p. 255.

Document 9: Frederick Douglass Praises the Emancipation Proclamation

In these passages from the October 1862 issue of his newspaper, Douglass'
Monthly, famous abolitionist Frederick Douglass is critical of Lincoln for acting too
slowly to end slavery, but he ultimately hails the Emancipation Proclamation as an
important step in the abolitionist cause. Douglass predicts the Southern reaction to
the proclamation and calls on the North to put a quick end to the coming war.

Common sense, the necessities of the war, to say nothing of the dictation of justice and humanity have at last prevailed. We shout for joy that we live to record this righteous decree. *Abraham Lincoln*, President of the United States, Commander-in-Chief of the army and navy, in his own peculiar, cautious, forbearing and hesitating way, slow, but we hope sure, has, while the loyal heart was near breaking with despair, proclaimed and declared: *"That on the First of January, in the Year of Our Lord One Thousand, Eight Hundred and Sixty-three, All Persons Held as Slaves Within Any State or Any Designated Part of a State, The People Whereof Shall Then be in Rebellion Against the United States, Shall be Thenceforward and Forever Free."* "Free forever" oh! long enslaved millions, whose cries have so vexed the air and sky, suffer on a few more days in sorrow, the hour of your deliverance draws nigh! Oh! Ye millions of free and loyal men who have earnestly sought to free your bleeding country from the dreadful ravages of revolution and anarchy, lift up now your voices with joy and thanksgiving for with freedom to the slave will come peace and safety to your country. President Lincoln has embraced in this proclamation the law of Congress passed more than six months ago, prohibiting the employment of any part of the army and naval forces of the United States, to return fugitive slaves to their masters, commanded all officers of the army and navy to respect and obey its provisions. He has still further declared his intention to urge upon the Legislature of all the slave States not in rebellion the immediate or gradual abolishment of slavery. But read the proclamation for it is the most important of any to which the President of the United States has ever signed his name. . . .

Whether slavery will be abolished in the manner now proposed by President Lincoln, depends of course upon two conditions, the first specified and the second implied. The first is that the slave States shall be in rebellion on and after the first day of January 1863 and the second is we must have the ability to put down that rebellion. About the first there can be very little doubt. The South is thoroughly in earnest and confident. It has staked everything upon the rebellion. Its experience thus far in the field has rather increased its hopes of final success than diminished them. Its armies now hold us at bay at all points, and the war is confined to the border States slave and free. If Richmond were in our hands and Virginia at our mercy, the vast regions beyond would still remain to be subdued. But the rebels confront us on the Potomac, the Ohio, and the Mississippi. Kentucky, Maryland, Missouri, and Virginia are in debate on the battlefields and their people are divided by the line which separates treason from loyalty. In short we are yet, after eighteen months of war, confined to the outer margin of the rebellion. We have scarcely more than touched the surface of the terrible evil. It has been raising large quantities of food during the past summer. While the masters have been fighting abroad, the slaves have been busy working at home to supply them with the means of continuing the struggle. They will not [back] down at the bidding of this Proclamation, but may be safely relied upon till January and long after

January. A month or two will put an end to general fighting for the winter. When the leaves fall we shall hear again of bad roads, winter quarters and spring campaigns. The South which has thus far withstood our arms will not fall at once before our pens. All fears for the abolition of slavery arising from this apprehension may be dismissed. Whoever, therefore, lives to see the first day of next January, should Abraham Lincoln be then alive and President of the United States, may confidently look in the morning papers for the final proclamation, granting freedom, and freedom forever, to all slaves within the rebel States. On the next point nothing need be said. We have full power to put down the rebellion. Unless one man is more than a match for four, unless the South breeds braver and better men than the North, unless slavery is more precious than liberty, unless a just cause kindles a feebler enthusiasm than a wicked and villainous one, the men of the loyal States will put down this rebellion and slavery, and all the sooner will they put down that rebellion by coupling slavery with that object. Tenderness towards slavery has been the loyal weakness during the war. Fighting the slaveholders with one hand and holding the slaves with the other, has been fairly tried and has failed. We have now inaugurated a wiser and better policy, a policy which is better for the loyal cause than an hundred thousand armed men. The Star Spangled Banner is now the harbinger of Liberty and the millions in bondage, inured to hardships, accustomed to toil, ready to suffer, ready to fight, to dare and to die, will rally under that banner wherever they see it gloriously unfolded to the breeze. Now let the Government go forward in its mission of Liberty as the only condition of peace and union, by weeding out the army and navy of all such officers as the late Col. [Dixon] Miles, whose sympathies are now known to have been with the rebels. Let only the men who assent heartily to the wisdom and the justice of the anti-slavery policy of the Government be lifted into command; let the black man have an arm as well as a heart in this war, and the tide of battle which has thus far only waved backward and forward, will steadily set in our favor. The rebellion suppressed, slavery abolished, and America will, higher than ever, sit as a queen among the nations of the earth.

Now for the work. During the interval between now and next January, let every friend of the long enslaved bondman do his utmost in swelling the tide of anti-slavery sentiment, by writing, speaking, money and example. Let our aim be to make the North a unit in favor of the President's policy, and see to it that our voices and votes, shall forever extinguish that latent and malignant sentiment at the North, which has from the first cheered on the rebels in their atrocious crimes against the union, and has systematically sought to paralyze the national arm in striking down the slaveholding rebellion. We are ready for this service or any other, in this, we trust the last struggle with the monster slavery.

Frederick Douglass, "The Emancipation Proclamation Is a Significant Achievement," in William Dudley, ed., *The Civil War*. San Diego: Greenhaven Press, 1995, pp. 180–86.

Document 10: Jefferson Davis Reacts to the Emancipation Proclamation

In this speech to the Confederate Congress on January 12, 1863, Confederate president Jefferson Davis expresses the Southern view that the Emancipation Proclamation was unjust. Moreover, Davis interprets the announcement as proof of the South's suspicions about Lincoln and as justification for secession. He argues that the proclamation will not end slavery but only make restoration of the Union impossible.

The public journals of the North have been received, containing a proclamation, dated on the 1st day of the present month [January 1863], signed by the President of the United States, in which he orders and declares all slaves within ten of the States of the Confederacy to be free, except such as are found within certain districts now occupied in part by the armed forces of the enemy. We may well leave it to the instincts of that common humanity which a beneficent Creator has implanted in the breasts of our fellowmen of all countries to pass judgment on a measure by which several millions of human beings of an inferior race, peaceful and contented laborers in their sphere, are doomed to extermination, while at the same time they are encouraged to a general assassination of their masters by the insidious recommendation "to abstain from violence unless in necessary self-defense." Our own detestation of those who have attempted the most execrable measure recorded in the history of guilty man is tempered by profound contempt for the impotent rage which it discloses. So far as regards the action of this Government on such criminals as may attempt its execution, I confine myself to informing you that I shall, unless in your wisdom you deem some other course more expedient, deliver to the several State authorities all commissioned officers of the United States that may hereafter be captured by our forces in any of the States embraced in the proclamation, that they may be dealt with in accordance with the laws of those States providing for the punishment of criminals engaged in exciting servile insurrection. The enlisted soldiers I shall continue to treat as unwilling instruments in the commission of these crimes, and shall direct their discharge and return to their homes on the proper and usual parole.

In its political aspect this measure possesses great significance, and to it in this light I invite your attention. It affords to our whole people the complete and crowning proof of the true nature of the designs of the party which elevated to power the present occupant of the Presidential chair at Washington and which sought to conceal its purpose by every variety of artful device and by the perfidious use of the most solemn and repeated pledges on every possible occasion. . . .

The people of this Confederacy, then, cannot fail to receive this proclamation as the fullest vindication of their own sagacity in foreseeing the uses to which the dominant party in the United States intended from the beginning to apply their power, nor can they cease to remember with devout thankfulness that it is to their own vigilance in resisting the first stealthy progress of approaching despotism that they owe their escape from consequences now apparent to the most skeptical. This proclamation will have another salutary effect in calming the fears of those who have constantly evinced the apprehension that this war might end by some reconstruction of the old Union or some renewal of close political relations with the United States. These fears have never been shared by me, nor have I ever been able to perceive on what basis they could rest. But the proclamation affords the fullest guarantee of the impossibility of such a result; it has established a state of things which can lead to but one of three possible consequences—the extermination of the slaves, the exile of the whole white population from the Confederacy, or absolute and total separation of these States from the United States.

This proclamation is also an authentic statement by the Government of the United States of its inability to subjugate the South by force of arms, and as such must be accepted by neutral nations, which can no longer find any justification in withholding our just claims to formal recognition. It is also in effect an intimation to the people of the North that they must prepare to submit to a separation, now become inevitable, for that people are too acute not to understand a restoration of the Union has been rendered forever impossible by the adoption of a measure which from its very nature neither admits of retraction nor can coexist with union.

Jefferson Davis, "The Emancipation Proclamation Is a Worthless Act," in William Dudley, ed., *The Civil War*. San Diego: Greenhaven Press, 1995, pp. 190–92.

Document 11: Lincoln Suspends the Writ of Habeas Corpus

Lincoln's suspension of the writ of habeas corpus was among his most controversial decisions. (The writ guarantees the right to a quick trial and prevents wrongful imprisonment or detention by legal authorities.) Lincoln issued this proclamation on September 24, 1862, two days after issuing the Emancipation Proclamation. Although some critics labeled him a tyrant for his decision, Lincoln insisted it was necessary to suppress Southern sympathizers living in the North who were obstructing the war effort. Congress validated the suspension in March 1863, and Lincoln followed it with a broader suspension that September.

Proclamation Suspending the Writ of Habeus Corpus
[September 24, 1862]
By the President of the United States of America:

A Proclamation.

Whereas, it has become necessary to call into service not only volunteers but also portions of the militia of the States by draft in order to suppress the insurrection existing in the United States, and disloyal persons are not adequately restrained by the ordinary processes of law from hindering this measure and from giving aid and comfort in various ways to the insurrection;

Now, therefore, be it ordered, first, that during the existing insurrection and as a necessary measure for suppressing the same, all Rebels and Insurgents, their aiders and abettors within the United States, and all persons discouraging volunteer enlistments, resisting militia drafts, or guilty of any disloyal practice, affording aid and comfort to Rebels against the authority of the United States, shall be subject to martial law and liable to trial and punishment by Courts Martial or Military Commission:

Second. That the Writ of Habeas Corpus is suspended in respect to all persons arrested, or who are now, or hereafter during the rebellion shall be, imprisoned in any fort, camp, arsenal, military prison, or other place of confinement by any military authority or by the sentence of any Court Martial or Military Commission.

In witness whereof, I have hereunto set my hand, and caused the seal of the United States to be affixed.

Done at the City of Washington this twenty fourth day of September, in the year of our Lord one thousand eight hundred and sixty-two, and of the Independence of the United States the 87th.

By the President: Abraham Lincoln
William H. Seward, Secretary of State.

Abraham Lincoln, "Proclamation Suspending the Writ of Habeas Corpus," in Mario M. Cuomo and Harold Holzer, eds., *Lincoln on Democracy*. New York: A Cornelia & Michael Bessie Book, 1990, p. 261.

Document 12: Lincoln Defends the Arrest of Clement L. Vallandigham

Following Lincoln's suspension of the writ of habeas corpus, thousands of Northerners were arrested for hindering the Union war effort. The most famous of these was Clement L. Vallandigham, who was arrested for treason after making numerous speeches against Lincoln's policies and urging peace negotiations with the Confederacy. In these excerpts from a letter Lincoln wrote on June 12, 1863, in response to a petition protesting Vallandigham's arrest, the president argues that his actions are justified in light of the national crisis.

He was not arrested because he was damaging the political prospects of the administration or the personal interests of the commanding general but because he was damaging the army, upon the existence and vigor of which the life of the nation depends. He was warring upon the military and this gave the military constitutional jurisdiction to lay hands upon him. If Mr. Vallandigham was not damaging the military power of the country, then his arrest was made on mistake of fact, which I would be glad to correct on reasonably satisfactory evidence. . . .

Long experience has shown that armies cannot be maintained unless desertion shall be punished by the severe penalty of death. The case requires, and the law and the Constitution sanction, this punishment. Must I shoot a simpleminded soldier boy who deserts, while I must not touch a hair of a wily agitator who induces him to desert? This is none the less injurious when effected by getting a father, or brother, or friend into a public meeting, and there working upon his feelings till he is persuaded to write the soldier boy that he is fighting in a bad cause, for a wicked administration of a contemptible government, too weak to arrest and punish him if he shall desert. I think that, in such a case, to silence the agitator and save the boy is not only constitutional but withal a great mercy.

If I be wrong on this question of constitutional power, my error lies in believing that certain proceedings are constitutional when, in cases of rebellion or invasion, the public safety requires them, which would not be constitutional when, in absence of rebellion or invasion, the public safety does not require them; in other words, that the Constitution is not in its application in all respects the same in cases of rebellion or invasion involving the public safety as it is in times of profound peace and public security. The Constitution itself makes the distinction, and I can no more be persuaded that the government can constitutionally take no strong measures in time of rebellion, because it can be shown that the same could not be lawfully taken in time of peace, than I can be persuaded that a particular drug is not good medicine for a sick man because it can be shown not to be good food for a well one.

Abraham Lincoln, "Vallandigham's Arrest Justified," in William Dudley, ed., *The Civil War.* San Diego: Greenhaven Press, 1995, p. 203.

Document 13: Lincoln's Actions Are Unconstitutional

The group of Ohio Democrats who protested the arrest of Clement L. Vallandigham, to whom Lincoln replied in Document 12, remained convinced that the president's actions were unconstitutional. In their June 26, 1863, response to Lincoln, parts of which are reprinted below, they maintain that freedom of speech and the press are indispensable in times of both war and peace.

Mr. Vallandigham may differ with the President, and even with some of his own political party, as to the true and most effectual means of maintaining the Constitution and restoring the Union; but this difference of opinion does not prove him to be unfaithful to his duties as an American citizen. If a man, devotedly attached to the Constitution and the Union, conscientiously believes that, from the inherent nature of the Federal compact, the war, in the present condition of things in this country, can not be used as a means of restoring the Union; or that a war to subjugate a part of the States, or a war to revolutionise the social system in a part of the States, could not restore, but would inevitably result in the final destruction of both the Constitution and the Union—is he not to be allowed the right of an American citizen to appeal to the judgment of the people for a change of policy by the constitutional remedy of the ballot-box? . . .

If the freedom of speech and of the press are to be suspended in time of war, then the essential element of popular government to effect a change of policy in the constitutional mode is at an end. The freedom of speech and of the press is indispensable, and necessarily incident to the nature of popular government itself. If any inconvenience or evils arise from its exercise, they are unavoidable. . . .

The undersigned are unable to agree with you in the opinion you have expressed, that the Constitution is different in time of insurrection or invasion from what it is in time of peace and public security. The Constitution provides for no limitation upon, or exceptions to, the guarantees of personal liberty, except as to the writ of *habeas corpus*. Has the President, at the time of invasion or insurrection, the right to engraft limitations or exceptions upon these constitutional guarantees whenever, in his judgement, the public safety requires it? . . .

The people of Ohio are willing to co-operate zealously with you in every effort warranted by the Constitution to restore the Union of the States, but they cannot consent to abandon those fundamental principles of civil liberty which are essential to their existence as a free people.

Ohio Democratic Convention, "Lincoln's Actions Violate Constitutional Liberties," in William Dudley, ed., *The Civil War*. San Diego: Greenhaven Press, 1995, pp. 196–200.

Document 14: Blacks Should Not Be Soldiers

Proposals to enlist blacks as soldiers in the Union army met with considerable opposition, especially from slave states that had remained in the Union. On July 9, 1861, Kentucky senator Garrett Davis, in this portion of a speech concerning a Senate proposal to enlist blacks into military service, expresses his view that blacks should be enlisted into the army as workers but not as soldiers.

I have myself never considered secession a remedy for any evil. I do not now consider it a remedy for any evil, but to have brought upon the country all existing evils; and that, if an accomplished fact, it would prove the fruitful mother of many other evils, of which we have yet had no experience. For my own State, for the South, for the North, for the East, and the West, I have no hope, if secession is triumphant and permanent dissolution takes place. I am for a reconstruction of the Union. I believe the only principle and means by which that reconstruction is possible, is by the employment of the full, legitimate military power of the country, and not by arming slaves and attempting to form a military force of them. . . .

From the debate that has sprung up in this Chamber on this subject, it appears to me that there are only two principal matters in the measure proposed about which there is much difference of opinion. The one is the employment of the negro in all camp and military labor, and the other is placing arms in his hands, and forming him into a portion of the soldiery of the United States in the war. To the first proposition I have no objection, and never had any, but to the second I am utterly opposed, and will ever be opposed. . . .

I never heard any Union man in my State or out of it object to the use and the appropriation of negroes by the United States Government, just as other property is applied to their military purposes. The whole of their remonstrance and protest has been against making a discrimination between that and other property by the laws of Congress or by the policy of the war, as the President or his generals might carry it on. When a general is commanding in the field, and he has occasion for the labor of horses and oxen, what does he do? He impresses them into the service of the Army of the United States, and nobody objects. Just so, if that general may need the services of negroes for the purpose of fortifying, or ditching, or rendering any other labor in his camp, or any service whatever, especially that kind which would shield and protect and save the life of the white soldier, I think that general in command would be perfectly authorized so to employ the negro, and I have never heard any man object to such employment; certainly I never made any such objection as that myself. And all this would be done by order of the President, or by our generals commanding, without any act of Congress to authorize it. But when the general has done with the negro, and the negro is no longer useful in his camp for the purpose of labor, or for any other useful purpose, let him be discharged, sent away like other property. I protest against placing arms in his hands and making a soldier of him; and to that line of policy I never will give my consent; nor will my people, although it may be regarded as a matter of very little importance in this Senate what they or I think in relation to this or any other measure of policy of the dominant party. . . .

Has it come to this, Mr. President, that we cannot command white soldiers enough to fight our battles to put down this rebellion? Whenever we authorize by law of Congress the enrollment of negro soldiers for that purpose, we admit that the white man is whipped in the contest, and that he cannot come out conqueror without making an auxiliary of the negro. I protest against any such degrading position as that. Our countrymen are not reduced to it; and sooner than the white men, the citizens and sovereigns of the United States, would submit to so humiliating an admission as that, one million of additional soldiers would be ready to rush to the battle-field. I believe that if this measure was passed it would weaken our Army; it would weaken the cause of the Union and of the legitimate Government in this contest tenfold as much as it would strengthen it.

Garrett Davis, "The Union Should Not Enlist Black Soldiers," in William Dudley, ed., *The Civil War.* San Diego: Greenhaven Press, 1995, pp. 214–16.

Document 15: Blacks Should Fight for the North

Alfred M. Green was a black schoolteacher and lecturer in Philadelphia who became involved in promoting the organization of black military units. In this excerpt from an article he wrote for the October 19, 1861, issue of the New York journal Anglo-African, *in response to an article from a previous issue, Green argues that the Civil War presents a tremendous opportunity for blacks to help free the slaves and prove their worth as American citizens.*

MR. EDITOR:

In your issue of September 28th, appears an able and elaborate article on the "Formation of Colored Regiments." I have no desire for contention at a time like this with those who differ honorably from me in opinion; but I think it just, once in a while, to speak out and let the world know where we stand on the great issues of the day, for it is only by this means that we can succeed in arousing our people from a mistaken policy of inactivity, at a time when the world is rushing like a wild tornado in the direction of universal emancipation. The inactivity that is advocated is the principle that has ever had us left behind, and will leave us again, unless we arouse from lethargy and arm ourselves as men and patriots against the common enemy of God and man. For six months I have labored to arouse our people to the necessity of action, and I have the satisfaction to say not without success. I have seen companies organized and under the most proficient modern drill in that time. I have seen men drilled among our sturdy-going colored men of the rural districts of Pennsylvania and New Jersey, in the regular African Zouave drill, that would make the hearts of secession traitors or prejudiced northern Yankees quake and tremble for fear.

Now I maintain that for all practical purposes, whatever be the turn of the war, preparation on our part, by the most efficient knowledge of the military art and discipline, is one of the most positive demands of the times. No nation ever has or ever will be emancipated from slavery, and the result of such a prejudice as we are undergoing in this country, but by the sword, wielded too by their own strong arms. It is a foolish idea for us to still be nursing our past grievances to our own detriment, when we should as one man grasp the sword—grasp this most favorable opportunity of becoming inured to that service that must burst the fetters of the enslaved and enfranchise the nominally free of the North. We admit all that has been or can be said about the meanness of this government towards us—we are fully aware that there is no more soul in the present administration on the great moral issues involved in the slavery question and the present war, than has characterized previous administrations; but, what of that; it all teaches the necessity of our making ourselves felt as a people, at this extremity of our national government, worthy of consideration, and of being recognized as a part of its own strength. Had every State in the Union taken active steps in the direction of forming regiments of color, we should now, instead of numbering eight regiments or about eight thousand five hundred men, have numbered seventy-five thousand—besides awakening an interest at home and abroad, that no vacillating policy of the half-hearted semi-secessionists of the North could have suppressed. . . .

The issue is here; let us prepare to meet it with manly spirit; let us say to the demagogues of the North who would prevent us now from proving our manhood and foresight in the midst of all these complicated difficulties, that we will be armed, we will be schooled in military service, and if our fathers were cheated and disfranchised after nobly defending the country, we, their sons, have the manhood to defend the right and the sagacity to detect the wrong; time enough to secure to ourselves the primary interest we have in the great and moving cause of the great American rebellion.

Alfred M. Green, "Blacks Should Fight for the North," in William Dudley, ed., *The Civil War*. San Diego: Greenhaven Press, 1995, pp. 226–30.

Document 16: The South Should Be Treated as a Conquered Nation

In December 1865 Congress established the Joint Committee on Reconstruction to make recommendations on policies concerning reconstruction. It was led by Senator Thaddeus Stevens, an outspoken proponent of radical reconstruction. The committee's June 20, 1866, report, portions of which are presented here, contends that the South is in effect a conquered nation and not entitled to constitutional guarantees or congressional representation. Many of the committee's resolutions were later incorporated into the Fourteenth Amendment.

A claim for the immediate admission of Senators and Representatives from the so-called Confederate States has been urged, which seems to your committee not to be founded either in reason or in law, and which cannot be passed without comment. Stated in a few words, it amounts to this: That inasmuch as the lately insurgent States had no legal right to separate themselves from the Union, they still retain their positions as States, and consequently the people thereof have a right to immediate representation in Congress without the imposition of any conditions whatever; and further, that until such admission Congress has no right to tax them for the support of the Government. It has even been contended that until such admission all legislation affecting their interests is, if not unconstitutional, at least unjustifiable and oppressive.

It is believed by your committee that all these propositions are not only wholly untenable, but, if admitted, would tend to the destruction of the Government.

It must not be forgotten that the people of these States, without justification or excuse, rose in insurrection against the United States. They deliberately abolished their State governments so far as the same connected them politically with the Union as members thereof under the Constitution. They deliberately renounced their allegiance to the Federal Government, and proceeded to establish an independent government for themselves. In the prosecution of this enterprise they seized the national forts, arsenals, dockyards, and other public property within their borders, drove out from among them those who remained true to the Union, and heaped every imaginable insult and injury upon the United States and its citizens. Finally they opened hostilities, and levied war against the Government.

They continued this war for four years with the most determined and malignant spirit, killing in battle and otherwise large numbers of loyal people, destroying the property of loyal citizens on the sea and on the land, and entailing on the Government an enormous debt, incurred to sustain its rightful authority. Whether legally and constitutionally or not, they did, in fact, withdraw from the Union and made themselves subjects of another government of their own creation. And they only yielded when, after a long, bloody, and wasting war, they were compelled by utter exhaustion to lay down their arms; and this they did not willingly, but declaring that they yielded because they could no longer resist, affording no evidence whatever of repentance for their crime, and expressing no regret, except that they had no longer the power to continue the desperate struggle. It cannot, we think, be denied by any one, having a tolerable acquaintance with public law, that the war thus waged was a civil war of the greatest magnitude. The people waging it were necessarily subject to all the rules which, by the law of nations, control a contest of that character, and to all the legitimate consequences following it. One of those consequences was that, within the limits prescribed by humanity, the conquered rebels were at the mercy of the conquerors. That a government thus outraged had a most perfect right to exact indemnity for the injuries done and security against the recurrence of such outrages in the future would seem too clear for dispute. What the nature of that security should be, what proof should be required of a return to allegiance, what time should elapse before a people thus demoralized should be restored in full to the enjoyment of political rights and privileges, are questions for the law-making power to decide, and that decision must depend on grave considerations of the public safety and the general welfare.

It is moreover contended, and with apparent gravity, that, from the peculiar nature and character of our Government, no such right on the part of the conqueror can exist; that from the moment when rebellion lays down its arms and actual hostilities cease, all political rights of rebellious communities are at once restored; that, because the people of a State of the Union were once an organized community within the Union, they necessarily so remain, and their right to be represented in Congress at any and all times, and to participate in the government of the country under all circumstances, admits of neither question or dispute. If this is indeed true, then is the Government of the United States powerless for its own protection, and flagrant rebellion, carried to the extreme of civil war, is a pastime which any State may play at, not only certain that it can lose nothing in any event, but may even be the gainer by defeat. If rebellion succeeds, it accomplishes its purpose and destroys the government. If it fails, the war has been barren of results, and the battle may be still fought out in the legislative halls of the country. Treason, defeated in the field, has only to take possession of Congress and the cabinet. . . .

The question before Congress is, then, whether conquered enemies have the right, and shall be permitted at their own pleasure and on their own terms, to participate in making laws for their conquerors; whether conquered rebels may change their theater of operations from the battlefield, where they were defeated and overthrown, to the halls of Congress, and, through their representatives, seize upon the Government which they fought to destroy; whether the national treasury, the army of the nation, its navy, its forts and arsenals, its whole civil administration, its credit, its pensioners, the widows and orphans of those who perished in the war, the public honor, peace and safety, shall all be turned over to the keeping of its recent enemies without delay, and without imposing such conditions as, in the opinion of Congress, the security of the country and its institutions may demand. . . .

The history of mankind exhibits no example of such madness and folly. The instinct of self-preservation protests against it.

The Joint Committee on Reconstruction, "Report of the Joint Committee on Reconstruction, 39th Cong., 1st sess., 1866," in Brenda Stalcup, ed., *Reconstruction*. San Diego: Greenhaven Press, 1995, pp. 39–42.

Document 17: Andrew Johnson Opposes Radical Reconstruction

Andrew Johnson sided with the Union after the Southern states seceded, but his views on race remained orthodox Southern. As president he fought many of the bills proposed by radical reconstructionists. In this extract from his March 23, 1867, message to Congress, Johnson explains his largely racial reasons for opposing Congress's plans for Reconstruction, especially black suffrage.

I repeat the expression of my willingness to join in any plan within the scope of our constitutional authority which promises to better the condition of the negroes in the South, by encouraging them in industry, enlightening their minds, improving their morals, and giving protection to all their just rights as freedmen. But the transfer of our political inheritance to them would, in my opinion, be an abandonment of a duty which we owe alike to the memory of our fathers and the rights of our children.

The plan of putting the Southern States wholly and the General Government partially into the hands of negroes is proposed at a time peculiarly unpropitious. The foundations of society have been broken up by civil war. Industry must be reorganized, justice reestablished, public credit maintained, and order brought out of confusion. To accomplish these ends would require all the wisdom and virtue of the great men who formed our institutions originally. I confidently believe that their descendants will be equal to the arduous task before them, but it is worse than madness to expect that negroes will perform it for us. Certainly we ought not to ask their assistance till we despair of our own competency.

The great difference between the two races in physical, mental, and moral characteristics will prevent an amalgamation or fusion of them together in one homogeneous mass. If the inferior obtains the ascendancy over the other, it will govern with reference only to its own interests—for it will recognize no common interest—and create such a tyranny as this continent has never yet witnessed. Already the negroes are influenced by promises of confiscation and plunder. They are taught to regard as an enemy every white man who has any respect for the rights of his own race. If this continues it must become worse and worse, until all order will be subverted, all industry cease, and the fertile fields of the South grow up into a wilderness. Of all the dangers which our nation has yet encountered, none are equal to those which must result from the success of the effort now making to Africanize the half of our country.

I would not put considerations of money in competition with justice and right; but the expenses incident to "reconstruction" under the system adopted by Congress aggravate what I regard as the intrinsic wrong of the measure itself. It has cost uncounted millions already, and if persisted it will add largely to the weight of taxation, already too oppressive to be borne without just complaint, and may finally reduce the Treasury of the nation to a condition of bankruptcy. We must not delude ourselves. It will require a strong standing army and probably more than $200,000,000 per annum to maintain the supremacy of negro governments after they are established. The sum thus thrown away would, if properly used, form a sinking fund large enough to pay the whole national debt in less than fifteen years. It is vain to hope that negroes will maintain their ascendancy themselves. Without military power they are wholly incapable of holding in subjection the white people of the South.

I submit to the judgment of Congress whether the public credit may not be injuriously affected by a system of measures like this. With our debt and the vast private interests which are complicated with it, we can not be too cautious of a policy which might by possibility impair the confidence of the world in our Government. That confidence can only be retained by carefully inculcating the principles of justice and honor on the popular mind and by the most scrupulous fidelity to all our engagements of every sort. Any serious breach of the organic law, persisted in for a considerable time, can not but create fears for the stability of our institutions. Habitual violation of prescribed rules, which we bind ourselves to observe, must demoralize the people. Our only standard of civil duty being set at naught, the sheet anchor of our political morality is lost, the public conscience swings from its moorings and yields to every impulse of passion and interest. If we repudiate the Constitution, we will not be expected to care much for mere pecuniary obligations. The violation of such a pledge as we made on the 22d day of July, 1861, will assuredly diminish the market value of our other promises. Besides, if we acknowledge that the national debt was created, not to hold the States in the Union, as the taxpayers were led to suppose, but to expel them from it and hand them over to be governed by negroes, the moral duty to pay it may seem much less clear. I say it may *seem* so, for I do not admit that this or any other argument in favor of repudiation can be entertained as sound; but its influence on some classes of minds may well be apprehended. The financial honor of a great commercial nation, largely indebted and with a republican form of government administered by agents of the popular choice, is a thing of such delicate texture and the destruction of it would be followed by such unspeakable calamity that every true patriot must desire to avoid whatever might expose it to the slightest danger.

Andrew Johnson, "President Johnson Vetoes Radical Reconstruction as an Invasion of States' Rights: Fears Amalgamation of Races and Africanization," in Harvey Wish, ed., *Reconstruction in the South, 1865–1877.* New York: Noonday Press, 1966, pp. 103–105.

CHRONOLOGY

1819
Missouri applies for admission to the United States as a slave state. Its status concerning slavery becomes an issue because its admission would upset the balance of eleven free states and eleven slave states that now compose the Union.

1820
Missouri Compromise passes Congress and is signed into law by President James Monroe. In addition to jointly admitting Missouri as a slave state and Maine as a free state, the law orders slavery excluded in all Louisiana Purchase lands north of 36°30' (except Missouri).

1850
Sen. Henry Clay launches the Senate debate on what will become the Compromise of 1850. California is admitted to the Union as a free state; New Mexico and Utah are admitted as territories, with the power to decide on their own whether to permit slavery ("popular sovereignty"); the slave trade is abolished in Washington, DC; and a new, tougher Fugitive Slave Law is enacted, with heavy penalties for those who interfere with the capture and return of escaped slaves.

1854
Kansas-Nebraska Act is passed in Congress, voiding the 1820 Missouri Compromise and potentially extending slavery into territories north of the 36°30' under the doctrine of popular sovereignty.

March 6, 1857
The Supreme Court decision of *Dred Scott v. Sandford* is announced; the Court rules that blacks are not citizens and therefore cannot bring suit in federal courts, that since slaves are property they may be taken anywhere in the United States without losing their slave status, and that the Missouri Compromise establishing a border between slave and free territory was unconstitutional. The decision is praised in the South and condemned in the North.

June 16, 1858
Abraham Lincoln of Illinois accepts the Republican nomination for U.S. senator; in his "House Divided" speech he declares that the United States cannot remain divided into slave and free sections.

November 1858
In congressional elections Republicans carry all Northern states except Indiana and Illinois; Douglas defeats Lincoln.

October 16, 1859
John Brown launches an unsuccessful raid on Harpers Ferry, Virginia, in the hope of triggering a general slave revolt. He and his followers are captured or killed by U.S. Marines. Brown is hanged on December 2 after being convicted of treason and conspiring with slaves to commit murder; he becomes a martyr in the eyes of many Northerners.

November 4, 1860
Abraham Lincoln wins the presidency with only 40 percent of the national popular vote but captures virtually all the electoral votes of the eighteen free states.

December 20, 1860
South Carolina, with a unanimous convention vote, becomes the first state to secede from the Union.

January 9, 1861
Mississippi secedes from the Union.

January 10–February 1, 1861
Florida, Alabama, Georgia, Louisiana, and Texas secede from the Union, while Kansas is admitted as a free state.

February 4–March 11, 1861
Delegates from the seven seceded states meet in Montgomery, Alabama, to form the Confederate States of America. They create a provisional Confederate Congress, write a constitution, and elect Jefferson Davis of Mississippi as provisional president and Alexander H. Stephens of Georgia as vice president. Davis is inaugurated on February 18, and selects a cabinet.

March 2, 1861
Congress adopts a proposed constitutional amendment guaranteeing no federal interference with slavery in slave states; the amendment is never ratified by the states.

March 4, 1861
Lincoln is inaugurated as the sixteenth president of the United States.

April 12, 1861
Confederate guns open fire on Fort Sumter.

April 14, 1861
The American flag is hauled down and the Confederate flag raised over Fort Sumter.

April 27, 1861
Lincoln suspends the writ of habeas corpus in portions of Maryland in order to permit the military arrests of suspected secessionists in this border slave state.

May 1861
Arkansas, Tennessee, and North Carolina join the Confederacy. The Confederacy now consists of eleven states with a population of 9 million (including 3.5 million slaves). Twenty-three states, with a population of 22 million, remain in the Union.

May 13, 1861
Great Britain, the leading world power, declares neutrality in the crisis, recognizing the Confederacy as a belligerent under international law but not as an independent nation.

July 4, 1861
Lincoln in a message to Congress reaffirms that he has "no purpose . . . to interfere with slavery in the states where it exists."

July 21, 1861
Confederate soldiers are victorious at the First Battle of Bull Run (Manassas).

August 6, 1861
Congress passes the First Confiscation Act, confiscating any property (slaves included) used directly in the Confederate war effort.

March 9, 1862
The world's first battle between two ironclad ships, the Union *Monitor* and the Confederate *Merrimack*, ends in a draw.

April 6–7, 1862
The Battle of Shiloh; Confederates launch a surprise attack against Grant's forces in Tennessee but are beaten back after two days' fighting that kills more people than all previous wars in American history combined.

April 16, 1862
The Confederate Congress enacts the first conscription law in American history.

July 17, 1862
Congress passes the Second Confiscation Act, which frees all slaves whose owners are rebelling against the United States and authorizes the president to "employ" blacks for the suppression of the rebellion.

September 17, 1862
The Battle of Antietam (Sharpsburg) results in about 12,000 casu-

alties for the North and 13,000 casualties for the South—the blood-iest day of the war. Lee is compelled to withdraw to Virginia, which gives Lincoln an opportunity to act on his emancipation plans.

September 22, 1862
Lincoln issues a preliminary Emancipation Proclamation, to take effect on January 1, 1863.

September 24, 1862
Lincoln suspends the writ of habeas corpus throughout the North and subjects "all persons discouraging voluntary enlistments" to martial law.

January 1, 1863
The Emancipation Proclamation takes effect. The proclamation in its final form lays more emphasis on the enlisting of black soldiers; by late spring, recruiting is under way throughout the North and Union-occupied areas in the South.

May 5, 1863
Democratic congressman Clement L. Vallandigham is arrested and tried for treason by military authorities; he is banished to the Confederacy on May 19.

July 1–3, 1863
The Battle of Gettysburg; 23,000 Confederate and 28,000 Union soldiers are killed, wounded, or missing in this Union victory; it marks the end of the last major Confederate offensive of the war.

November 19, 1863
Lincoln delivers his Gettysburg Address.

November–December 1864
General Sherman marches his army across Georgia to the Atlantic Ocean, destroying Southern economic resources and morale.

November 8, 1864
Lincoln is reelected, carrying all but three states.

January 31, 1865
Congress approves the Thirteenth Amendment to the Constitution to abolish slavery by a vote of 119–56; amendment is sent to states for ratification.

March 13, 1865
The Confederate Congress passes a measure authorizing enlist-ment of black troops, with an implied promise of freedom for slaves who serve.

April 9, 1865
Lee surrenders to Grant at Appomattox Court House.

April 14, 1865
Lincoln is assassinated by John Wilkes Booth, a Confederate sympathizer; Andrew Johnson assumes presidency.

December 13, 1865
Thirteenth Amendment to the Constitution, abolishing slavery, is ratified by the states.

STUDY QUESTIONS

Chapter 1

1. In what American documents do secessionists find justification for breaking up the Union? In what American documents do Unionists find a counter argument? Which of these documents, if any, should take precedence over the others and settle the debate over the appropriateness of secession?

2. According to the secessionist opinions expressed in Viewpoint 1, which legislative body should determine whether slavery should be permitted in a state? According to the Unionist opinions expressed in Viewpoint 2, which legislative body should make that decision? Compare the reasons given for these two distinct views.

3. Proponents and opponents of slavery often relied on the same principles—for example, God's law or the U.S. Constitution—to make opposing arguments. Which side makes the more persuasive argument and why?

4. Southerners often accused Northerners of having hidden motives in their efforts to abolish slavery. What were those motives, according to slavery proponents, and how important were they in the overall slavery debate?

Chapter 2

1. In the debate over the Emancipation Proclamation, supporters predicted it would be a great boost to the Northern war effort while detractors contended it would have lasting damage for the Union cause. On what basis does each side make these opposing claims, and who makes the stronger argument?

2. Neither supporters nor opponents of the Emancipation Proclamation believed the proclamation would forestall war. In fact, it probably incited passions on both sides. Given this result, was its issuance a wise decision?

3. Abraham Lincoln believed that a president had broader powers during times of war than during times of peace. Is this an acceptable position? Why or why not, and under what conditions?

4. According to Thomas Wentworth Higginson in Viewpoint 9, what are some of the advantages that black soldiers have over their white counterparts? Why do men like Garrett Davis in

Viewpoint 10 feel that some of these "advantages" may prove to be detrimental to healing the nation?

5. In Viewpoint 10, why was President Lincoln initially reluctant to organize regiments of black combat soldiers?

Chapter 3

1. Why do advocates of radical Reconstruction believe they are justified in using their political power to reshape the South, regardless of whether the Southerners welcome the changes?

2. Why does President Johnson resist granting African Americans the right to vote and other civil rights? According to his view, how, if at all, will blacks be afforded these rights?

3. In Viewpoint 12, what does Thaddeus Stevens fear will happen to Congress if blacks are not given the right to vote?

FOR FURTHER READING

Henry Steele Commager, ed., *The Blue and the Gray: The Story of the Civil War as Told by Participants*. New York: Bobbs-Merrill, 1950. Excellent compilation of primary documents that relate a variety of opinions on both military and nonmilitary aspects of the war.

William Dudley, ed., *The Civil War: Opposing Viewpoints*. San Diego: Greenhaven Press, 1995. A collection of mostly primary source documents showing alternative opinions on different issues that arose during the Civil War era.

William Dudley, ed., *Slavery: Opposing Viewpoints*. San Diego: Greenhaven Press, 1992. A collection of mostly primary source documents showing alternative opinions on slavery during the colonial and antebellum periods of American history. Viewpoints range from moral arguments to political debates.

Eric Foner, *A Short History of Reconstruction, 1863–1877*. New York: Harper & Row, 1990. An abridged version of Foner's award-winning book *Reconstruction: America's Unfinished Revolution*. Foner's writing is engaging as he traces the political and economic motivations that impinged on the plans for Reconstruction.

John Hope Franklin and Alfred A. Moss Jr., *From Slavery to Freedom: A History of African Americans*. New York: Alfred A. Knopf, 1994. A compact history of blacks in America. Slave narratives and reminiscences of black soldiers during the Civil War are of particular interest.

Milton Meltzer, ed., *Voices from the Civil War: A Documentary History of the Great American Conflict*. New York: Thomas Y. Crowell, 1989. A collection of documents and speeches pertaining to the war. The work is aimed at young readers.

Brenda Stalcup, ed., *Reconstruction: Opposing Viewpoints*. San Diego: Greenhaven Press, 1995. A collection of mostly primary source documents showing alternative opinions on issues relating to Reconstruction. The introduction gives a compact description of the major differences between President Johnson's plan for Reconstruction and the radical Republicans' counter strategy.

Kenneth M. Stampp, ed., *The Causes of the Civil War*. Rev. ed. New York: Simon & Schuster, 1974. A varied collection of primary and secondary sources giving views on issues that separated the

North and the South. Documents include editorials, speeches, and analyses by postwar historians.

Geoffrey C. Ward with Ric Burns and Ken Burns, *The Civil War: An Illustrated History.* New York: Alfred A. Knopf, 1991. The companion volume to Ken Burns's PBS documentary on the Civil War. Filled with pictures and firsthand accounts.

ADDITIONAL WORKS CONSULTED

Bruce Catton, *The Coming Fury.* Vol. 1 of *The Centennial History of the Civil War.* Garden City, NY: Doubleday, 1961. Part of Catton's excellent overview of the Civil War era. Catton focuses on dissolution of the Union, including some of the causes and the immediate repercussions of secession. The remaining volumes in this series are also valuable resources.

Avery Craven, *Reconstruction: The Ending of the Civil War.* New York: Holt, Rinehart, and Winston, 1969. Like other historians of the period, Craven attempts to show that the end of the Civil War did not signal the end of the issues that had caused the conflict. His presentation is straightforward and contends well with the discrepancies between President Johnson's plan and the Republican's push for radical Reconstruction.

Mario M. Cuomo and Harold Holzer, eds., *Lincoln on Democracy.* New York: A Cornelia & Michael Bessie Book, 1990. Essays by prominent historians discuss the writings and speeches of Abraham Lincoln.

David Brion Davis, *Antebellum American Culture: An Interpretive Anthology.* University Park: Pennsylvania State University Press, 1997. Primary source documents exemplify the attitudes of the North and the South during the prewar period. Discussions focus primarily on cultural distinctions but include abolitionism, religious differences, and political beliefs.

John Hope Franklin, *The Emancipation Proclamation.* Garden City, NY: Doubleday, 1963. A readable discussion of the events surrounding the proclamation's adoption and the controversies that preceded and followed.

Hondon B. Hargrove, *Black Union Soldiers in the Civil War.* Jefferson, NC: McFarland, 1988. A good examination of the role of black soldiers in the Union army. Deals with the prejudices faced by black enlistees and the bravery they exhibited during combat. Many firsthand accounts enliven the narrative.

Jeffrey Rogers Hummel, *Emancipating Slaves, Enslaving Free Men: A History of the American Civil War.* Chicago: Open Court, 1996. A sweeping narrative history of the Civil War and an examination of the war's significance for American society.

James M. McPherson, *Battle Cry of Freedom: The Civil War Era.* New York: Ballantine Books, 1989. Landmark work by a leading

Civil War historian. This thick volume encompasses the war years and provides an abundance of firsthand commentary.

————, *Drawn with the Sword: Reflections on the American Civil War.* New York: Oxford University Press, 1996. A short collection of essays that examine several topics relating to the war. The essays are narrowly focused, thus, the work is not meant to be comprehensive.

————, *Ordeal by Fire: The Civil War and Reconstruction.* New York: Alfred A. Knopf, 1982. The war and its aftermath are examined in another of McPherson's well-known works.

Mark E. Neely Jr., *The Fate of Liberty: Abraham Lincoln and Civil Liberties.* New York: Oxford University Press, 1991. Though Neely does not paint Lincoln as a dictator, he does examine many of the president's tamperings with and suspension of civil liberties.

————, *The Last Best Hope of Earth: Abraham Lincoln and the Promise of America.* Cambridge, MA: Harvard University Press, 1993. An examination of Lincoln coming to power and wielding presidential authority. Showing Lincoln's evolution in the political arena is Neely's strength.

Page Smith, *Trial by Fire.* Vol. 5 of *A People's History of the Civil War and Reconstruction.* New York: McGraw-Hill, 1982. The volume of *A People's History of the Civil War and Reconstruction* that deals with the war years. Smith's work is exhaustive and provides a highly detailed examination of the war.

Kenneth M. Stampp, *The Era of Reconstruction, 1865–1877.* New York: Alfred A. Knopf, 1965. Less in-depth than some other sources, Stampp's book is nonetheless clear in presenting the scope of political issues surrounding Reconstruction.

Richard Taylor, *Destruction and Reconstruction: Personal Experiences of the Late War.* 1879. Reprint, New York: Time-Life Books, 1983. An interesting narrative on the Civil War and Reconstruction by a former lieutenant-general in the Confederate army.

Harvey Wish, ed., *Reconstruction in the South, 1865–1877.* New York: Noonday Press, 1966. An excellent collection of primary source documents from the era of Reconstruction. All the major players are represented in this anthology.

INDEX

abolition
  government control is reason for,
    51–52
  legislation on, 10
  martyrdom through, 11–12
  and Southern economy, 33–34, 48–49
African Americans
  after Civil War, 27–28
  conditions for, South vs. North, 50–51
  equality for, 43–44, 93
    con, 49–50
  freedom of, catastrophe of, 49
  oppose black soldiers in combat, 84
  retribution for, 92
  voting rights for, 27–28, 89
  war should not be fought for, 84–85
  see also slavery; soldiers, black
Afro-American, 79
agriculture, 48
Alabama, 12
American Anti-Slavery Society, 43
Antietam, Battle of, 17
Appomattox Court House, 25
Arkansas, 14
Army of the Potomac, 19–20
Atlanta, 23–24
Atlantic Monthly, 22

Baltimore, 72
Bibb, Henry, 42–43
Bible
  opposes slavery, 41–42
  supports slavery, 50
Bledsoe, Albert Taylor, 48
border states, 18
  arrest of civilians in, 75–76
  divisions over slavery in, 15
  slavery ignored in, 57
  see also states
Breckenridge, John C., 38
Brown, George, 14–15
Bull Run, Battle of, 15

Calhoun, John C., 10, 32
California
  as free state, 10
Chancellorsville, 18
Chase, Salmon P., 59–60
chattel slavery, 41
  see also slavery
Chicago Journal, 39
Cincinnati Daily Commercial, 38

civilians, arrest of, 73
  complaints about, 69
  reasons for, 75–76
  for small crimes, 67
civil rights
  Constitution does not ensure, 89–90
  legislation on, 27–28
  Lincoln violates, 67–69
  must be given to African Americans, 93
Civil Rights Act of 1866, 27
Civil War
  casualties, 18
  mobilizing army for, 14–15
  see also Confederate army; North;
    South; Union army
Compromise of 1850, 10, 33
Confederate army, 14, 15, 23–25
  battles of, 15–17, 19–21
  inadequate supplies for, 18–19, 22
  surrender of, 25–26
Confederate States of America, 12
Constitution
  civil rights for African Americans in,
    89–90
  does not protect slavery, 43–44
  presidential powers in, 14–15
  purpose of, 36–37
  and right to hold slaves, 34
  secession is treason against, 37

Davis, Garrett, 84–85
Davis, Jefferson, 18–19, 23
  on benefits of slavery, 50
  on Emancipation Proclamation, 55–56
Declaration of Independence, 31
Delaware, 15
Douglas, Stephen, 11
Douglass, Frederick, 63
  on black soldiers, 62, 80
  on meaning of Constitution, 44
  on voting rights for blacks, 94

Emancipation Proclamation, 17–18
  on black soldiers, 83–84
  Europe opposes, 57
  Europe supports, 62–63
  goal of, is to ruin Southern economy,
    60–61
  is morally right, 63
  Southern response to, 55–56
  will save the Union, 59, 60
    con, 54–55

ABOUT THE AUTHORS

David Haugen is the managing editor of Greenhaven Press. He holds a master's degree in English literature and has worked as an author, editor, and instructor.

Lori Shein is an editor and writer. She has edited books for young readers for the past eight years. Before becoming an editor, she spent ten years reporting and writing for newspapers. She lives in San Diego, California.